SPY HIGH

A Dolphin Book
Doubleday

New York London Toronto Sydney Auckland

A
S P Y
BOOK

S P Y
HIGH

A Make-Believe Yearbook of America's Rich and Famous

**by Jamie Malanowski, Susan Morrison
and the Editors of SPY**

**Art Direction by
Alexander Isley Design**

**Written and Edited
by Jamie Malanowski, Susan Morrison
and the Editors of SPY**

**Art Direction by
Alexander Isley Design, *New York***

Principal Photography by Marina Garnier

Photo Research by Nicki Gostin

Typography by Patrick Miller Design, New York

Contributors:	Henry Alford
	Aimée Bell
	Tom Gammill
	Josh Gillette
	Joanne Gruber
	David Kamp
	T.P. Moynihan
	Matthew Tyrnauer

Principal Bush's letter by George Kalogerakis

A Dolphin Book
PUBLISHED BY DOUBLEDAY
A division of Bantam Doubleday Dell Publishing Group, Inc.
666 Fifth Avenue, New York, New York 10103
DOLPHIN, DOUBLEDAY, and the portrayal of the two dolphins
are trademarks of Doubleday, a division of Bantam
Doubleday Dell Publishing Group, Inc.

Library of Congress Cataloging-in-Publication Data
Malanowski, Jamie.
Spy high: a make-believe yearbook of America's rich and famous / by Jamie Malanowski.
Susan Morrison, and the editors of Spy. – 1st ed.   p.   cm.   "A Dolphin book."
1. Celebrities–United States–Humor. 2. Parodies.
I. Morrison, Susan   II. Spy (New York, N.Y.)   III. Title.   PN6231.C25M35 1991
817'.5408–dc20   91-10783   CIP
ISBN 0-385-41100-6

Contents

Alma Mater

We hail our alma mater,
We hold her banner high,
We dareth not besmirch its hem,
We do not knoweth why.
We see its tasteful colors,
Glowing black and blue,
Our hearts are yours forevermore,
Alma Mater, we are you.

Thy children, Alma Mater,
Are the fairest in the land,
What Nature has denied them,
They take from surgeon's hand.
With implants and reductions,
Tucks, eye-lifts and the rest,
We'll resist all signs of aging,
And always look our best.

Thy rules of fame and fortune
That we studied at your knee
Will serve us well in thick and thin,
As we seek publicity.
The art of spin control
Is something we've learned well,
We'll command attention where e'er we are,
Stage, screen or prison cell.

The quest for riches, Mater,
We fight with fang and claw,
With shameless manipulations,
But most times within the law.
Where e'er the money comes from—
Inherited, paid or lent—
Between jewelry, jets and legal fees
We'll spend it, every cent.

Long life for Alma Mater,
Rule on forevermore,
Vanquish all who would compete,
Destroy them by the score.
We'll stay on top forever,
And ride first-class only,
We're your sons and daughters for all time,
O Alma Mater, we love thee.

Office of the Principal

SPY HIGH

You're all—there you are—and you're all in graduation mode. And congratulations. You're leaving school who has been your home for years. For four years. Something of that nature. And I know that that's an awful lot. And I hope, and the faculty and administration and staff, that they've—I've—we've—imparticated to you all the dedication and commitment to loyalty and honesty and virtue. And for not just in the short term. Virtuoso citizens.

As graduating seniors, the sense of values that you have are great. Remember when you were freshmen? But with the sophomore year, and then juniors—the values better and better all the time. But not until this previous year did you put it all together—all the values and the learning and the growing and the aspirationing that you have had into one. That has been some year. And we hang our hats to you.

And on your experience at SPY High, I hope that the bad stuff—and it has been a little on both sides, let's just say it, maybe not .compassion and understanding over here, maybe too much incompletions and late slips over the other way. And also—hey, we're having our cards all over the table now—let's recall all the disciplinary action that has been necessary, on our part about you. And so again, on this even very, very bad stuff, it will hopefully all be reversed into something that's positive. Positive from the experience—on your reflection, in that regard. Because is there one senior among you that can honestly say—or one faculty—"My behavior has always been 110 percent blameless"? No. Nor I.

In the future you will face goals and problems. I can assure you that there's no easy answers—in terms of rules of thumb—on how to do it, this concept of a responsive mode. Of really being right there, out there, sending out those signals loud and clear, to meet those challenges. No certain answers—assure you of that. Hypothecate? In a moment.

And now those thumb rules. Because there's a booklet, even in life, a little stapled thing with the rules, no matter if it's horseshoes. Or, yes, life. Three—there's three of them. And there's a warning here, and that is that they're only rules—on how to play it out in the world in your future careers. But I'm just going to send them out and let them sit out there and whatever you want to do, happens. Okay.

One: Recreate. Tee up. Volley for serve. On your marks. Start your engines. Fish and cut bait. Think I know what I'm talking about here.

Two: Follow the rules. These rules right here.

And these rules—you're not gonna believe—well, the rules say now that I'm out of space. That that's all the space. I know, the third one, the rule—but I'm afraid that that's all the space that I have. And now I have to go back in there. Go back in there to go to work. God bless SPY High, and good luck. Back into my office.

George H. W. Bush

Who made those rude noises in assembly?

D-uh! Artiste Sylvester Stallone after leaning into one of his paintings that hadn't dried yet.

Time it was, and what a time it was, in the halls of Spy High

School ombudsman Mr. Dinkins goes out stylin'. He's still the freshest!

When the Biology Department ran out of frogs this year, perky Maria Conchita Alonso was the lucky freshman assigned to dissect a giant iguana.

For this year's spring trip, chaperoned by Coach Schwarzenegger, students traveled to Central Europe and were offered the opportunity to discuss current events with respected world leaders.

Don't worry, Paul, you won't always be a little freshman weenie. One day you'll show 'em!

Sophomore Gilbert Gottfried demonstrating how a guy as short and gnarly as himself can be so popular.

Freshmen Emily Lloyd and Balthazar Getty make the scene in the cafeteria. *Go for it, dude!*

Freshman L.L. Cool J displays a decorative weapon he made himself in Mr. Gingrich's Metal Shop Class.

Junior Billy Joel, just as Mr. Sununu was grabbing his ear for a one-way trip to Principal Bush's office.

The hilarious Danny A. of the junior class says: "What's this about seniors being horny, Chevy?"

"Teach us to care and not to care;
teach us to sit still."
—T. S. Eliot

FACULTY

Mr. Bush, *Principal*

Mr. Giuliani, *Vice Principal and Dean of Discipline*

Mr. Dinkins, *Ombudsman*

Mr. Powell, *Head of Security*

Mr. Vidal, *Head Librarian*

Mrs. Westheimer, *School Nurse*

Miss Rivers, *School Secretary*

▶ Deeply involved in the life of the school, Principal Bush is a hands-on administrator whose door is always open to students. Here he towels off a pig.

Mr. Dinkins observes juniors Meryl Streep and Joanne Woodward participating in a Parapsychology Class experiment in extrasensory perception. ▼

Vice Principal Giuliani, accompanied by hall monitor Al D'Amato of the senior class, prepares for a spot inspection of the second-floor lockers. ▶

Mr. Alda, *Guidance Counselor*

Mr. Liman, *Career Adviser*

Mr. Donahue *"...And this is your brain on drugs."*

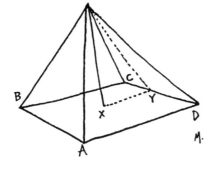

Mrs. Helmsley

Mr. Tisch

Mr. Souter

Mr. Sununu

◄ At a teachers' conference, Mr. Tisch masks his dismay at the discovery that popular student teacher Miss Sawyer has brought a date.

Mrs. Schroeder

Mr. Nader

Mr. Scott

Mr. Jobs, *Teaching Assistant*

Mr. Henley, *Student Teacher*

Looking for unhealthy palm-oil products, Mr. Trillin does a spot check of the teachers'-lounge refrigerator.

Ms. Ellerbee

Mr. Lish

Miss. Sawyer, *Student Teacher*

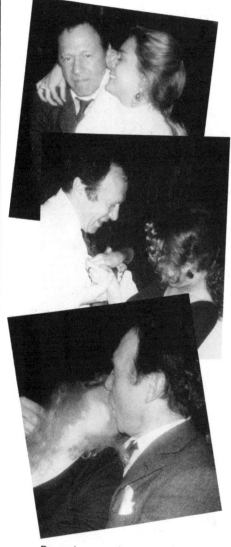

Mr. Shawn, *Department Chairman Emeritus*

Mr. Haden-Guest, *Visiting Poet*, and Mr. Plimpton

Poetry's never been so popular with certain segments of the student body as it has si... the arrival of visit-... ...Mr. Haden-Guest!

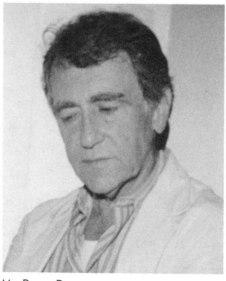

Mr. Papp, *Drama*

Mr. Franklin, *Speech Therapist*

Though semiretired, Mr. Shawn generously shares his thoughts on literature and plastic purses with members of the student body—in this case, senior Bob Gottlieb. ➤

"Why, yes, Stumpy, I guess Shakespeare *would have been wealthy if he could have written for the movies.*" Mr. Plimpton discusses issues in literature with senior Henry Kravis.

Art and Music Departments

&

Mr. Berry, *Music*

Mr. Sondheim, *Music*

Mr. Castelli, *Art*

Mr. Helms, *Aesthetics*

Mr. Hamilton, *Spanish*

Miss Collins, *French*

Miss Gabor, *Hungarian* (with junior Merv Griffin)

Mr. O'Connor, *Latin*

Mr. Kempton, *Director, Language Laboratory*

"La via del tren subterraneo es muy peligrosa," says Señor Hamilton. "Oui, oui," replies Mademoiselle Collins.

Mrs. Thatcher

Mr. Schwarzenegger

Miss Moore

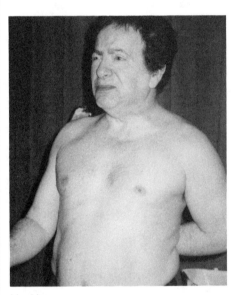

Mr. Mason

Mr. Steinbrenner

On a sad note, this spring we marked the retirement of Mr. Melman, longtime coach of the girls' swim team.

◄ "Von day you'll get up da rope, Dahnny." Mr. Schwarzenegger offers encouragement to spunky sophomore Danny DeVito.

Ms. Redgrave

Mrs. Kirkpatrick

Mr. Safer

Mr. Kissinger

Mr. Moynihan

As senior George Will waits to ask a question about American Cold War policy, Mr. Kissinger pretends to sit enraptured as junior Roberta Peters pretends to play a Mozart sonata on her purse.

Mr. Haig

Industrial Arts

Mr. Goldstein, *Wood Shop*

Mr. Hefner, *Print Shop*

Mr. Gingrich, *Metal Shop*

Home Economics

Mrs. Brown poses with one of her star students, junior Erica Jong, here showing off a fantasy in floral polycotton blend that she sewed herself.

Mrs. Brown, *Sewing*

Mr. King, *Cooking*

Mr. Dukakis is a stickler for the rules of the road. He teaches what he calls *passive road conduct:* "When an 18-wheeler is headed right for you, remember to check all mirrors and dashboard instruments before making any potentially dangerous evasion decisions. Auto safety is very important, very important. Fifty-five saves lives. It does. And I believe that."

Mr. Dukakis, department chairman

An ounce of prevention is as good as an ounce of, uh, something else. Here, juniors Tom Selleck and Jilly Mack practice the "bend-forward-and-tuck" sequence designed by Mr. Dukakis to mitigate serious head injuries in the event that a student is involved in an Intoxicated Chauffeur incident.

The right way to exit a stretch limo, demonstrated by Coach Schwarzenegger...

...And the wrong way, demonstrated by jumbo junior Marvin Davis.

SPY High students don't drive their cars themselves very often—thus the Driver's Ed emphasis on safe and courteous back-seat entrance and exiting techniques. Here, after successfully executing the cab-hailing part of his assignment, Stumpy Kravis does a tricky door-opening maneuver and helps his steady, Carolyne, into the backseat.

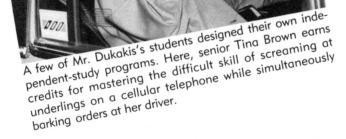

A few of Mr. Dukakis's students designed their own independent-study programs. Here, senior Tina Brown earns credits for mastering the difficult skill of screaming at underlings on a cellular telephone while simultaneously barking orders at her driver.

Mrs. Kempner, *Typing*

Mrs. Adams, *Shorthand*

Does the man ever sleep? Because his students don't really care about learning what goes on behind the wheel of a car, Mr. Dukakis has lots of time on his hands to help out other folks. Here, the always helpful Mr. D. lends a hand to the SPY High groundskeeping staff—note the protective lawnmowing gloves.

Mr. Koch, *Bus Driver*

Miss Smith, *Cafeteria Lady*

Mr. Lewis, *Cafeteria Manager*

Mr. List, *Custodian*

◄ *"Maybe the best cafeteria lady, in terms of quality, that the world has ever seen!"* Miss Smith doubled as senior-class adviser and won many admirers.

SENIORS

Mario Cuomo, *president*
Jane Pauley, *vice president*
Mike Milken, *treasurer*
Mort Zuckerman, *secretary*
Miss Smith, *faculty adviser*

Senior Superlatives

MOST RESPONSIBLE
Jane Pauley and Bill Bradley

CLASS ORATOR
Al Sharpton

COOLEST
Jack Nicholson

MOST AMBITIOUS
Mike Ovitz and Tina Brown

NO, VOTE FOR ME!

VOTE FOR ME

BEST GROOMED
Calvin Klein and
Georgette Mosbacher

BEST COUPLE
Jane Fonda and Ted Turner

GAVE MOST WEDGIES
Don "Stinky" Trump

PHYS. ED.

PHYS. ED.

GOT MOST WEDGIES
Woody Allen

BIOLOGY

CREEPIEST
Stephen King

CLASS BRAINIACS
George Will and Susan Sontag

CLASS LOTHARIO
AND MOST POPULAR GIRL
Warren Beatty and Madonna Ciccone

MOST MEMORABLE WAY
OF SPEAKING
Barbara Walters

THRIFTIEST Bill Cosby

CLASS WEASEL
Al D'Amato

Senior Superlatives

PARTY ANIMALS
Jay McInerney and Sylvia Miles

BEST DANCERS
Mick Jagger and
Sandra Bernhard

MOST LIKELY TO EXPERIENCE A STRESS-RELATED DISORDER
Marilyn Quayle

FIRST TO MAKE A MILLION
Madonna Ciccone

FIRST TO MARRY A MILLION
Gayfryd Steinberg

MOST LIKELY TO SUCCEED
Ivana Trump and John Gotti

MOST SENSITIVE
Gordon "Stinger" Sumner and Barbra Streisand

MOST DETERMINED
Yoko Ono and Mort Zuckerman

MOST CHANGED SINCE FRESHMAN YEAR
Cherilyn Sarkasian

WOODY ALLEN

"Man is sometimes extraordinarily, passionately in love with suffering and that is a fact."
—Dostoevsky

"The Woodman"...Freshman-year nebbish, senior-year brain...*His latest projects show he's no dummy/ But we liked him better when he was funny.* Just kidding...Why so secretive?...DK *and* MF? Who woulda thunk?...Goal: work in Sweden
Cinephiles 2,3,4; Calliope 2; National Honor Society; Jazz Band 2,3,4

ROSEANNE BARR

I'm outta here.

"Rosey"...Famous whiner and diner...Don't call her jolly...Kicked out of choir...Never forget good times hangin' at the caf
Slimnastics 1; A/V Squad 3,4; Thespian Society 3; Girls Mud Wrestling 4

SYDNEY BIDDLE BARROWS

*"I think passing love around
Is all we were born to do."*
—Doobie Brothers

"Madam"..."Need a prom date, guys?"...Honors for her home-delivery project for Junior Achievement...Love that lineage!... Ambition: a career in PR
Sadie Hawkins Dance Committee; Publicists of Tomorrow 4; Junior Achievement 3,4; Helping Hands 2

Seniors

WARREN BEATTY

"If you can't be with the one you love, love the one you're with."—Stephen Stills

"Don." Or "Juan"..."Ah. Uuuummmmm"...So vain?...Remember: the 150-page freshman term paper he finally turned in—senior year?..."You should apply yourself more often, Mr. Beatty"...Remembers special times with IA, BB, CB, LC, C, JC, CC, FD, BE, DH, GH, KJ, DK, VL, M, CM, MP, DR, JS, DS, CS, BS, NW; Ambition: presidential adviser
Cinephiles 1,2,3,4; Girls Swim Team manager 1; Twirlers manager 2; Girls Gymnastics manager 3,4; Young Democrats 3

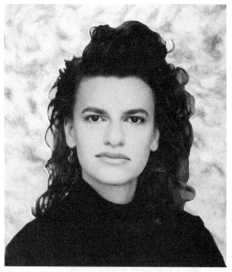

SANDRA BERNHARD

"I can suck melancholy out of a song as a weasel sucks eggs."—Shakespeare

"Lips"..."Don't Hate Me Because I'm Beautiful." *Right.* (Just kidding).
Calliope 1,2 (poetry editor),3,4; Synchronized Swimming 1

CARL BERNSTEIN

"Meet me in the field, behind the dynamo."
—Bruce Springsteen

"Carlo"...Boss loafers...Co-recipient in his freshman year of the Rookie Reporter Prize. What've you done since then, Carl? (Just kidding!)...Now, what is it that Nora E. says about you and venetian blinds?...Won: New Jersey Award—for spending so much time in Elizabeth...Ambition: to be important enough to get free invitations to nightclubs
Ping-Pong Club 1; Junior Decorators 1,2,3,4; Dance to Help El Salvador 2; The Mercury (reporter) 1,2,3,4

TINA BROWN

" 'What is the use of a book,' thought Alice, 'without pictures or conversations?' "
—Lewis Carroll

"Lotta Headlights"...Just Wild About Harry (especially when he was more important)..."Guess who *I'm* having dinner with?"...Loves: *People* magazine, old movie stars of the 1970s, Tab, the philosophy of Dale Carnegie...Boy-crazy?..."What do you mean, 'the little people'?"...Ambition: to be on a first-name basis with lots of important celebrities
Thespian Society 1; Twirlers 2; The Mercury 2; Calliope 3,4

BILL BRADLEY

"And the men who hold high places must be the ones to start to mold a new reality closer to the heart."—Rush

"Dollar Bill"...Starting forward on SPY High's championship b-ball squad..."Uh-oh, No-Doz time—Bill's got his hand up again!"...*A guy so tall just had to play ball/ But he'd do more scoring if he weren't so boring.* Just kidding..."I bet a girl as cute as you has a lot of fresh ideas about the federal budget deficit"
Basketball 1,2,3,4 (captain); Student Council 3,4; Economics Club 3,4; National Honor Society 2,3,4

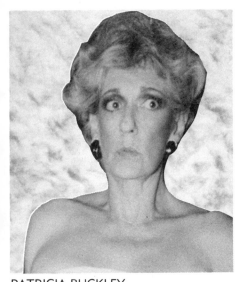

PATRICIA BUCKLEY

*"People try to put us down
Just because we get around."*—the Who

"Beanstalk"..."Oh, Bill's just kidding around. He thinks tattoos are tacky"...Will always remember: bringing her first makeup kit to school—how's that hernia, Pat?..."Tell me, Patricia, do you just want to be a social butterfly all your life?" Goal: marriage
Basketball 1; Helping Hands 2,3; Thespian Costume Committee 2,3; Sophomore Spring Fling chairman 2; Homecoming Dance 3; Prom chairman 4

Would you like to share it with the class, mister? And writing in school books is not allowed! Roseanne Barr makes the best of library detention with boyfriend Tom Arnold.

WILLIAM F. BUCKLEY JR.

"All that is not me is incomprehensible."
—Louis Aragon

"Bill"..."Don't use big words, Mr. Buckley, unless you know what they mean"...We'll always remember: the wild snippets from his diary that appeared in *Calliope*: "It is only a quarter to twelve, but suddenly I am ravenous, and so I head for the cafeteria for a croque monsieur. I take a minute to peruse *The Wall Street Journal*, then take out my portable computer and polish off my assignment for English class, a 250-word theme on the poverty of neoliberalism. It takes about eight minutes, only because I am distracted when Norman Mailer insists on pushing up next to me and using his hand to make flatulence noises in his armpit right by my ear. What a delightful colleague! Then Pat arrives. She has some carrots and talks about how she and Gay are going shopping together so they won't wear the same thing to the prom. I remind her about sweat shields."
Student Council 1; Debate Society 1,2,3,4 (president); Calliope 1,2,3,4; Young Americans for Freedom 1,2,3,4; Junior Yachtsmen 1,2,3,4

DAVID BYRNE

"It's a beautiful day in the neighborhood."
—Mister Rogers

"Geekster"..."This ain't no disco!"..."Neat"... "Wipe that smirk off your face, Mr. Byrne!"...Can't dance...Hey Dave—your clothes don't fit!...Ambition: ethnomusicology
Ping-Pong Club 1; Yearbook art department 1,2; Band 2,3; Love the Planet Society 4; Ethnomusicologists Я Us 4.

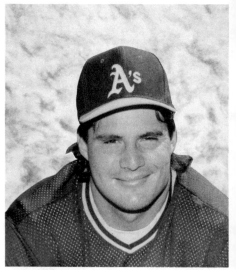

JOSE CANSECO

Thanks, Mom and Dad.

"Hulk"...Star slugger of school championship baseball team...AURGHH!...Hold that temper..."I don't want a man who belongs to a club, but a man with a club that belongs to him! Find me a primitive man!" (Cole Porter)..."Steroids? Never! I swear!"
Skeet Shooting 3; Baseball 1,2,3,4

CHEVY CHASE

"What, me worry?"—Alfred E. Neuman

"Smoothie"...Will never forget: mucho good times in the boys' room sophomore year...Lives for vacations...Ambition: "Just to be the best at something"
A/V Squad 1; Tennis 2,3; Cinephiles 2,3,4

MADONNA LOUISE CICCONE

"Purity is the ability to contemplate defilement."—Simone Weil

"No, it's just 'Madonna' "..."Like a virgin" (yeah, right—good memory)... Brought out the beast in SP, the butch in SB, the dork in WB...Prizes: her girlfriends... Spits out: boys...Nice, uh, cones..."I'm going to be in charge of my, y'know, life, okay?"... Ambition: unlimited
Chorus 1,2,3,4; Jazzercise 1,2; Photo Club (model) 1; Thespian Society 3,4; Cinephiles 3,4; Young Marketing Geniuses 1,2,3

WILLIAM F. COSBY

"I am a millionaire. That is my religion."
—George Bernard Shaw

"Cos"…Three-letter athlete…Class Cheapskate…Will do anything for a buck…"Because it's *my* money"…Goal: more money, more diplomas

Football 1 (JV),2,3,4; Track 2,3,4; Basketball 2,3,4; Boxing 2,3; Cinephiles 3,4; Young Speculators 2,3,4; Black Students Union 4

MARIO CUOMO

"Each of us bears his own hell."—Virgil

Led debate team to tournament victories for four years, yet always refused to go to the Nationals…Hey, lighten up, MC!… Remembers: senior social-studies paper, "Why the Mafia Doesn't Exist"… Forced out of the Cardinal Neumann Society—he was pro-girls'-right-to-wear-halter-tops-to-school.

Baseball 1; Basketball 1; St. Cardinal Neumann Society 1; Thomas More Society 2,3,4; Student Council 4 (president); Debate Society 1,2,3,4 (captain)

ALFONSE D'AMATO

To T.P., B.D., Sal, Sonny, Armand, Vinnie at the Pizza Parlor, Hal, Mr. Brainard, Lou at the pool, Lou at the gas station, and Father O'Connor—you're the best. AAAYYYYY!!! I MADE IT.

"Fonzo"…"Howyadoin'?"…Cherishes: memories of after-school job allocating lockers and student parking permits…"See Fonzo. Offer him two dollars"…Not as dumb as he looks—we hope…Goal: civil service

Football 1; Road Rally Committee 4

ROBERT DE NIRO

"Bobby"

BARRY DILLER

"Nice guys finish last."—Leo Durocher

"Killer"…BD and DVF sittin' in a tree, or what?…Fond memories of: producing the *Folies de SPY High*, cycle club outings with Mr. Forbes (R.I.P., dude), and that freaky summer night with Bianca and Calvin. Ambition: to look bitchin' in leather pants

Cycle Club 2,3,4; Young Speculators 2,3; Cinephiles 3,4; Big Brothers 3,4

Seniors

SAM DONALDSON

"Intellect is invisible to the man who has none."—Schopenhauer

"Yakety Yak"..."Stop shouting, Mr. Donaldson, and raise your hand like everyone else"...Favorite phrase: "But—, but—"
Ping-Pong Club 1; Trekkies 2 (vice president); A/V Squad 1,2,3; Debate Society 2,3,4

MICHAEL EISNER

"Be somebody. Know that a bunch of guys will do anything you tell 'em. Have your own way or nothin'."—Edward G. Robinson in *Little Caesar*

"Goofy"...Just a big kid!...Treasures: memories of playing with mice in biology lab...Goal: work for Art Linkletter
Mascot Committee 1,2; JV Basketball 1; Junior. Achievement 1,2,3,4; Young Democrats 3,4; Cinephiles 2,3,4

NORA EPHRON

"It's not true that life is one damn thing after another—it's the same damn thing over and over again."—Edna St. Vincent Millay

"Gummy"..."Marijuana is the pesto of high school."...Men seldom make passes at girls who, uh, have no tits and flat asses (yeah, yeah—quit complaining!)...Watch it, guys, she has a special technique for getting back at creeps..."If you can't say something nice about someone, Miss Ephron, don't say anything at all"
The Mercury 1,2,3; Cinephile Bake Sale Committee 4; Prom Committee 4

Senior Sam Donaldson and student teacher Miss Sawyer pose in front of the construction-paper mural he's just completed as his final project in her Tolstoy course. Sam thinks he's one of her favorite pupils.

LOUIS FARRAKHAN

No.

"Bow Tie"..."Keep your pop quiz, you white devil!"...Cherishes the independent-study project he did with Patrick Buchanan of the junior class: "Adolf Hitler: On the Other Hand"..."You could all learn a thing or two about neatness from Mr. Farrakhan!"... Big Junior Achievement success with his "Clean 'n Fresh" line of male grooming aids
Debate Society 1,2,3,4; Black Students Union 1,2,3,4; Junior Achievement 4

JANE FONDA

"Each of us is in truth an idea of the Great Gull, an unlimited idea of freedom"—Richard Bach

"Jane"…Feel the burn!…The feistiest Thespian…Active in Student Council (at least until Tom H. graduated—just kidding!)…"Ho, Ho, Ho Chi Who?"…Remember how she came back so much, well, *bouncier* after Christmas vacation last year?
Pep Club 1; Cheerleader 2; Thespian Society 1,2,3,4; Student Council 2,3; Elizabeth Cady Stanton Coven 3; Slimnastics 2,3,4; Junior Achievement 3,4; Love the Planet Society 4

JOHN GOTTI

Goodbye to my friend Mr. Giuliani. We will meet again, dirtbag.

"Don"
Helping Hands 3,4

ROBERT GOTTLIEB

"I'm a steam roller, baby, a churnin' urn of burnin' funk"—Elvis Presley

"Bobster"…Inherited editorship of *Calliope*… Carried his books around in an old Soupy Sales lunchbox…"That's not junk, those are rare and valuable collectibles"… Goal: to never wear a tie
Diaghilev Society 1,2 (president); Flea Marketeers 1,2,3,4; Calliope 3,4; National Honor Society 1,2,3,4

BRYANT GUMBEL

"Charm is a way of getting the answer yes without having asked any clear question."—Camus

"Bry"…Dumped Jane for Debbie and ended up with Joe. Bummer…Likes: Cubs, golf, himself. Hates: his mom, Willard S. (Just kidding!)…"Would you like to share your opinions with the rest of the class, Mr. Gumbel? I thought not"….Motto: Live for Today
A/V Squad 2,3,4; St. Cardinal Neumann Society 2,3,4; Football 1; Golf 2,3,4

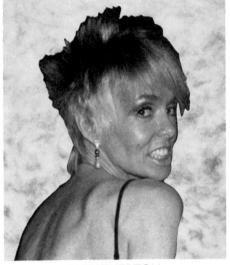

JOSEPHINE HEATHERTON

"I will survive! I will survive!"—Gloria Gaynor

"Joey"
Chorus 1; Twirlers 1, 2

Seniors

JESSE JACKSON

"A thought is often original, though you have uttered it a hundred times."—Oliver Wendell Holmes

"The Rev"…"I am somebody!" (for sure) …The Main Man at pep rallies: "Defense! Defense! That's no jive! Kick some butt! Keep hope alive!"…Why'd he suck up in Driver's Ed? …Ambition: to be principal of SPY High **Debate Society 1,2; Black Students Union 1,2,3,4; Bible Study Group 1,2; Cheerleading 2,3,4 (cheer consultant); Helping Hands 1,2,3,4**

MICHAEL JACKSON

"And I must borrow every changing shape to find expression."—T. S. Eliot

"Earth to Michael, Earth to Michael"…Known for: far-out Science Fair projects—junior year: "The Amazing, Changing Me"; senior year: "My Skeleton Collection"…Loves: Elizabeth, Bubbles, epaulets, powerful grown-ups. Hates: air, germs, dry hair, other grown-ups **Drum Major 2,3; Trekkies 1,2,3,4; Mascot Committee 3**

MICK JAGGER

"The bigger the bankroll, the bigger the rubber band."—Anon.

For a buck, he'll do that thing with his tongue…Strange walk…First student to have his own manor house…Ambition: live in a tax haven with a bimbo who talks funny **Boys Gymnastics 1; Band 2; Young Speculators 3,4**

EDWARD KENNEDY

"How dry I am. How wet I'll be, if I don't find the bathroom key."—Trad.

"Teddy"…He gets around…*He's got Jack's charm and Bobby's fervor/ But if he drives you home, bring a life preserver. (Just kidding!)*…"Come out from underneath that cafeteria table, Mr. Kennedy, and bring your friend with the pompoms with you!"…Loves: chicks, boilermakers, his family …Ambition: to be 175 pounds, U.S. president, or commodore of Hyannisport Yacht Club **Student Council 1,2,3,4; Debate Society 2; Tennis 2,3,4; Football 1,2**

STEPHEN KING

"Sickness is just slang for doing something somebody else wouldn't do."—Prince

Gross me out!…Loves: the smell of formaldehyde in biology lab ("But Steve, it's not dead yet!")…Hates: stuck-up prom-queen types…Motto: Quantity, Not Quality…Goal: career in forensic medicine **Ping-Pong Club 1,2; Komputer Klub 1; Trekkies 1,2; Tolkien Society (founder) 2,3,4; Cinephiles 1,2; Love the Planet Society 3**

MICHAEL KINSLEY

"The worst of doing one's duty was that it apparently unfitted one for doing anything else."—Edith Wharton

"Weenie"…Teacher's pet…Youngest-ever editor of *The Mercury*…Watches lots of TV for a smart guy…Nicely groomed…*In scholarship he's beyond compare/ But wake up, Mike, there's girls out there!* (Just kidding)…Ambition: teach political science
Ping-Pong Club 1; The Mercury 1,2,3; Debate Society 2,3,4; National Honor Society 1,2,3,4; Young Democrats 1,2,3,4; Young Republicans 4

CALVIN KLEIN

"Shall I part my hair behind? Do I dare to eat a peach?
I shall wear white flannel trousers, and walk upon the beach."—T. S. Eliot

Loves: WASPs, double-breasted jackets, the Bee Gees… Motto: "If obsession is a sin, then let me be guilty." *Huh?*…Gives his girlfriend Kelly an allowance…Ambition: to ride a horse without looking scared
Art Club 1,2; Junior Achievement 2,3,4

KEVIN KLINE

"The play's the thing."—Shakespeare

"All the world's a stage, even the cafeteria. *Particularly* the cafeteria"…Cherishes: memories of senior drama project, his three-hour one-man show, *The Bard 'n' Me*…Ambition: to mount on-Broadway Kevin Kline production of *Hamlet*, directed by and starring Kevin Kline
Thespian Society 1,2,3,4 (president)

HENRY KRAVIS

"I think no virtue goes with size."—Emerson

"Runtulus"…"Money is no object—so lend me some!" …Will he ever find out what's on the top shelf of his locker? …Mucho big spender on girlfriend Carolyne R…."Hey, Stumpy!"…"I don't care what they do in New York City, Mr. Kravis—the art studio is a place for classwork, not for throwing parties!"
Junior Achievement 1,2,3,4 (president); Helping Hands 4

RALPH LAUREN

"As if his whole vocation were endless imitation."—Wordsworth

"Mr. Abercrombie"…Favorite season: autumn…Tried to organize a school cricket team sophomore year—c'mon… Loves: cowboy-and-Indian movies, *McHale's Navy*, Redford as Gatsby, the L.L. Bean catalog…Excelled at tracing in art class
Rugby (JV) 1; Golf (JV) 1; Lacrosse (JV) 2; Girls Field Hockey 3 (manager); Equestrian Club 3,4 (manager)

FRAN LEBOWITZ

"Yesiree, I was smokin' in the boys' room."—Brownsville Station

Bitch, bitch, bitch, party, party, party, bitch, bitch, bitch…"Hey, Fran, we don't have a dress code here"…"Miss Lebowitz, this is not an essay that you have turned in—this is a *list*"…Most Talkative
The Mercury 1

DAVID LETTERMAN

"The fact is I am quite happy [at] a movie, even a bad movie. Other people, so I have read, treasure memorable moments in their lives."—The Moviegoer

"Dave"...An eternal dilemma: geek, clown or jerk?..."If you can't get up in the morning, Mr. Letterman, try going to bed earlier!"...Watermelon-seed-spitting ace...Ambition: "To goof off all day and get paid for it"
Baseball 1; The Mercury 1; Ham Radio Club 3,4 (president)

SHIRLEY LORD

"It is no use to blame the looking glass if your face is awry."—Nikolai Gogol

"Wench"..."Come on, Abe honey, loosen up!"...Idols: Nancy Sinatra, Judith Krantz..."Miss Lord, math class is not the place for using your eyelash curler"...Sophomore Science Project: "You and Your Pores"...Junior Science Project: "Our Friend the Sun Block"...Senior Science Project: "Mr. Penis and Ms. Clitoris Say Hello"...Voted the Girl Most Likely to Attract a Crowd of Boys While Doing Jumping Jacks
Future Secretaries of America 1; Domestic Science Club 1,2,3; Prom Committee

DAVID LYNCH

"Someone left the cake out in the rain."—Richard Harris

"Mr. Gross-Out"..."Hey, let's go to Dunkin Donuts" ...Always trying to find out what's in those locked custodian's closets...*He's quiet and quirky, a square type of fella/ But he's doing something right if he had Isabella!*...Gym class laughingstock...Loves: caffeine, anthills, picking scabs...Ambition: undecided
Ping-Pong Club 1; Tolkien Society 1; Cinephiles 1,2,3,4; Scouting 1,2,3,4; Young Republicans 2; Calliope 2,3

Seniors

SHIRLEY MACLAINE

"I'll be back."—The Terminator

One of the only cute girls who never dated Warren B...Mouth in the gutter, head in the clouds..."I'm sorry, Miss MacLaine, but a footnote citing 'Personal Experience' isn't sufficient in a history term paper"
Thespian Society 1,2,3,4; Jazzercise 2,3; Cinephiles 1,2,3,4; Chorus 1,2; Geology Club 3

NORMAN MAILER

"What is moral is what you feel good after."—Hemingway

"Fug!"..."Five hundred words only, Mr. Mailer. I have 28 papers to grade"..."She's all right, but she's no Marilyn"...Riunite rules!...No More Bullsh-t...Remembers: food fights, postgame parties...Ambition: write the Great American Novel
Boxing 1; Student Council 2; Helping Hands tutoring program 2; Cinephiles 3; Calliope 1,2,3,4; Prom Committee 4

JAY MCINERNEY

"In a real dark night of the soul it is always three o'clock in the morning."—F. Scott Fitzgerald

"You"…"So where's the party?"…blues buff…Will never forget The Boys (Hey Morgan, pass the mousse!)…Why so sniffly?…"I bet you're thinking of becoming an actress. Me? I'm a writer"…Ambition: work at *The New Yorker*
Calliope 1

SYLVIA MILES

"I want to rock and roll all night, and party every day."—Kiss

Party girl…Can usually be found: in the girls' room with Shirley L. applying still more make-up…Nachos!…Always an inspiration to anyone who feels inhibited about wearing clothes that might be considered too trendy or too, uh, tight
JV Cheerleading 1; Thespian Society 1,2,3,4

MICHAEL MILKEN

"I will gladly pay you Tuesday, for a hamburger today."—Wimpy

"Mike"…"Trust me"…"Some men see things as they are and ask why, other men dream dreams that never were, and ask whether there isn't a dollar in there somewhere"… Class of '91 mystery: why such a rich guy would have such an awful rug
Class Treasurer 4

JOSEPH MONTANA

"Choose a job you love, and you will never have to work a day in your life."—Confucius

"Joe"…Notre Dame on his mind…*Jumping from traction back into action was more than a little chancy/ But worse is his life, which, wife after wife, he lives as a passing fancy.* Just kidding, Cap'n!
A/V Squad 4; Football 1,2,3,4 (captain)

Senior Jane Fonda made 100 of these life-size Valentines to send to all the cutest, richest boys in school. The message: "Feel the burn, Valentine!"

GEORGETTE MOSBACHER

"Leave them while you're looking good." —Anita Loos

"Georgie Girl"…Great teeth—are they yours?…The homecoming queen that might have been…"A girl should wear a little make-up—unless she wants to become an old maid"…Treasures: memories of slow dancing with Ivana, er—Bob…Ambition: hand modeling

JV Cheerleading 2,3; Homecoming Committee 1,2,3; Prom Committee 4; Junior Achievement 2,3,4 (president); Young Republicans 4

RUPERT MURDOCH

"Show me a thoroughly satisfied man and I will show you a failure."—Thomas Edison

"Rupe"…"Do we really need all these people?"…Known for: super-catchy titles on his term papers…"C'mon, guys, it's exaggerating, not lying"… Ambition: just try to appeal to peoples' better instincts

Calliope 1,2; The Mercury 1,2,3,4; A/V Squad 3,4

EDDIE MURPHY

"There's no such thing, you know, as picking out the best woman: it's only a question of comparative badness."—Plautus

"Haygh! Haygh! Haygh!"…"Get those bitches out of here!"…Prizes (and pays): beefy friends…Small problem being, uh, *influenced* by other students' work…Wishes he could sing…Ambition: to star in movies as memorable as Dean Martin's Matt Helm series

A/V Squad 1; Class Vice President 2

Seniors

BILL MURRAY

"Fearlessly the idiot faced the crowd smiling."—Pink Floyd

"Billy"…"That's the fact, Jack!"…When did Domino's deliver that face? (Just kidding)… Unpredictable…Class Clown…Loves: helping out the ladies in the cafeteria, baseball, "99 Bottles of Beer on the Wall" anyplace, anytime…Ambition: job with the post office in Hawaii

Baseball 1,2; A/V Squad 1,2; Cinephiles 2,3,4; Helping Hands 2,3,4

PRINCE ROGERS NELSON

Thank U, God.

"His Royal Badness"…Even as a four-foot-tall freshman, had his eye on the prettiest girls in the senior class…Drove the English teachers nuts: "I would die 4 U," "U don't have 2 B rich 2 B my girl"…Never forget making funky music with KB…Ambition: actor-director-writer-musician-philosopher

Band 1,2,3,4; Calliope 2; Chorus 1,2,3; Twirlers 2,3

SAMUEL I. NEWHOUSE JR.

"I live for my dreams and a pocketful of gold."
—Led Zeppelin

"Si"…Has his hands in all school publications…Early riser…Loves: lumpy crewnecks, buying stuff…Sucker for: British accents…Goes through friends fast
Mathletes 1,2,3; The Mercury (treasurer) 3,4; Calliope (treasurer) 3,4; Yearbook (treasurer) 3,4

MIKE NICHOLS

"Funny is in the eye of the beholder."
—Garfield

"Chihuahua"…Brainy but popular…DS forever, even if her ratings bite it…Virginia Woolf fan
Thespian Society 1,2; Cinephiles 1,2,3,4

JACK NICHOLSON

"In my life, I've loved them all."—the Beatles

Jack be nimble!…Heartbreaker…Hey, nice tongue…Take off the shades, already!…Exercise regimen includes 100 eyebrow arches a day…Coolest…Ambition: to own a really big car
Basketball (manager) 1,2; Cheerleader 3,4; Cinephiles 1,2,3,4

YOKO ONO

"No bird soars too high, if he soars with his own wings."—William Blake

"The Yokester"…Artsy-fartsy…Is fond of: big apartments…"Cover your ears, Yoko's gonna sing!" (Just kidding!)
Art Club 1,2; Band, 3; Calliope 2,3,4 (president); Junior Rolfers 2; Young Speculators 3,4; Love the Planet Society 4

"Hey doll, check this out. I made it into *Remedial Reading!*" Good going, Andy Silverstein!

MICHAEL OVITZ

" 'Do other men for they would do you.' That's the true business precept."—Charles Dickens

"The Manipulator"…"Try that, pal, and you'll never get anywhere in this school"…No comment…Admires: loyalty…Most Serious… Ambition: law school
A/V Squad 1,2,3; Helping Hands 4; Cinephiles 4; *Folies de SPY High* **(talent coordinator) 4**

JANE PAULEY

"Just call me angel of the morning." —Juice Newton

"Janie"…What a nice girl!…"No, that's the way my hair's *supposed* to look"
The Mercury 1,2; Pep Club 1,2,3; National Honor Society 1,2,3,4; Helping Hands 1,2,3; Homecoming Committee 2,3

MARILYN QUAYLE

"Genius is one percent inspiration and ninety-nine percent perspiration."—Thomas Edison

Teacher's pet…"You are so immature!"… Favorite moods: bossy, high-strung…Ambition: "Oh, just to go to college and to law school, and meet a nice boy, and have kids, and a career, and all the responsibilities and pressures of adulthood"
National Honor Society 1,2,3,4; Library Bake Sale 1,2,3,4; Prom Committee 3,4 (Decorations Committee co-chairperson); Field Hockey 1,2,3,4

"For God's *sake*, buy some *cake*, what a difference you can *make*!" No one brought as much verve to senior-class bake sales as Jesse Jackson!

DAN RATHER

"What a long, strange trip it's been." —Grateful Dead

"Kenneth"…Temper, temper!…Customary breakfast: a jelly donut and 12 cups of coffee …Famous for six-minute disappearing acts…What *is* the frequency?…Motto: Courage. (Huh?)
The Mercury 1,2,3,4

ABRAHAM M. ROSENTHAL

"I should not talk so much about myself if there were anybody else whom I knew as well." —Thoreau

"Abe"...*Abie Baby*/ *In his years at High*/ *Kissed the girls*/ *And made them cry* (separate occasions, mind you)..."Hey Shirl! Ooga Chucka, Ooga Chucka!"...Video nites...Motto: "Without Fear or Favor, but Let's Not Get Ridiculous"..."I-I-I-I-I"...That's no haircut, that's a police composite! (Just kidding!) **The Mercury 1,2,3 (editor); Prom Committee 4**

STEVEN ROSS

"You never know what is enough unless you know what is more than enough."—William Blake

"Steverino"..."This is going to be BIG!"...Everybody's pal...Don't: ask him to play video games..."I don't care what you say about 'synergy,' Mr. Ross—you may not merge Cinephiles with the literary magazine!"...Ambition: to run a funeral parlor. Or a parking lot. Or a powerful global communications conglomerate **Junior Achievement 1,2,3,4; Cinephiles 3,4 (secretary-treasurer); Chorus 3,4 (secretary-treasurer)**

CHERILYN SARKASIAN

"She's got a lot of pretty, pretty boys that she calls friends."—the Eagles

"Cher"..."Hey, Cher, Halloween was *months* ago!"...Has provided a lot of hands-on guidance to selected members of the freshman class (what?)...Ambition: to work at a perfume counter **Pep Club 1; Cinephiles 3,4**

JULIAN SCHNABEL

"My mother and your mother were hanging up clothes.
My mother punched your mother right in the nose.
What color blood came out?"—Anon.

"El Tubbo"...Nachos! ...*Big* Man on Campus (just kidding!)...Would rather die than smile...Hey, Julian, aren't you a little young to write your memoirs?...Goal: to be friends with important maître d's **Ping-Pong Club 1; Cycle Club 2,3,4; Art Club 2,3,4**

AL SHARPTON

"Perhaps there is no happiness in life so perfect as the martyr's."—O. Henry

"The Mound of Sound"...*Al has got the pompadour*/ *And disposition sunny*/ *What we all would like to know is,*/ *Where'd he get the money?*...Got his photo in every issue of *The Mercury*..."You gonna finish those fries?"...OUTRAGEous! **Grooming Club 1; Wrestling 1; Bible Study Group 1; Junior Achievement 1; Black Students Union 2,3,4**

ANDREW SILVERSTEIN

"We all are born mad. Some remain so." —Samuel Beckett

"The Crapsman"...Hey, TORPEDO!...Thinks he's a *real* greaser...*Some may say that Andy's brilliant*/ *Some think he's a wit*/ *But everyone who's met him knows*/ *He's just a piece of*...Voted Boy Most Likely to Have an Accident in the Lavatory **Komputer Klub 1; A/V Squad 1,2,3; Cycle Club 4**

CURTIS SLIWA

"While we sit and we talk and we talk and we talk some more, someone's brother lies bleeding in a gutter somewhere."—Phil Collins

"Cur-TIS"...Wore the same shirt for four years...Hat, too
Hall Monitors 1,2,3,4

SUSAN SONTAG

"The question is, said Alice, whether you can make words mean so many different things."—Lewis Carroll

"The Brain"...As smart as any teacher (now where do we go to pick up our diplomacy award?)...Double 800's?...Girl Most Likely to Ruin the Grading Curve
National Honor Society 1,2,3,4; Cinephiles 2,3; Calliope 2,3,4

STEVEN SPIELBERG

"That's all, folks"—Porky Pig

"Spiels"...Neato..."Grow up, Steve!"..."I saw a movie about that once"..."Awards presentations are shallow anyway"
Tolkien Society 1,2; Trekkies 2,3,4; A/V Squad 1,2; Cinephiles 1,2,3,4

Seniors

SYLVESTER STALLONE

"Where's the beef?"—Clara Peller

"Sly"..."Yo!"...Volunteered his body for a Science Club experiment...Loves: painting ("It's the real me"), musk oil, Irish coffee
Boxing 1,2; Art Club 3,4; Cinephiles 1,2,3

GAYFRYD STEINBERG

"I just adore a penthouse view. Darling I love you, but give me Park Avenue."—Eva Gabor

"Saul—you're chewing too loudly again, honey"...Remember: the superextravagant party she threw for SS, and everybody came whether they liked him or not?...Tried to make friends with the gang at *Calliope*...Favorite song: "Diamonds Are a Girl's Best Friend" (oh—you *hate* that song. Our mistake!)
Helping Hands 2,3,4; Prom Committee 4

SAUL STEINBERG

"Hey hey mama, like the way you move. Gonna make you sweat, gonna make you groove!"—Led Zeppelin

"Porky"...Last in gym class to finish the mile. Last picked for intramural basketball. First cut in football. Never made it up the rope..."I will own you all one day"...Will GS ever give him the combination to the lock on the fridge?...Favorite song: "Can't Buy Me Love" (oh—that's your *least* favorite song. Our mistake!)
Junior Achievement 2,3,4; Helping Hands 4

GLORIA STEINEM

"I am woman. Hear me roar."—Helen Reddy

Often dated, never pinned...Looks the same as she did freshman year... Ambition: to have it all
Elizabeth Cady Stanton Coven 1,2,3; Prom Committee 4; The Mercury 1,2,3,4

BARBRA STREISAND

"Nobody gets too much heaven no more, it's as high as a mountain and harder to climb."—the Bee Gees

"Babs"..."How come when a guy acts like me he's called a perfectionist, but when a girl acts like me, she's called a bitch?"...Yes, it *is* large, but you can still kiss her... Will never forget true love with Jon and Don.
Chorus 1,2,3,4; Cinephiles 2,3,4; Young Democrats 3,4

GORDON SUMNER

"The progress of an artist is a continual self sacrifice, a continual extinction of personality."—T. S. Eliot

"Stinger"...King of Pain, King of Schmain!...Student Most Likely to Misuse Big Words in Public...Ambition: to be really, really liked by the black students
Band 1,2,3,4; Thespian Society 4; Love the Planet Society 4

ELIZABETH TAYLOR

"Never economize on luxuries."—Angela Thirkell

"Miz Liz"...Motorcycle mama!..."No, I shouldn't, I'm on a diet. But maybe just this once"...Didn't date much, but went steady fast...Memories: those weekends in New York with CB
Slimnastics 3; Cinephiles 1,2; Helping Hands 3,4

LAWRENCE TAYLOR

"Talk low, talk slow, and don't say too much."—John Wayne

"LT"…SPY High's all-around best athlete…Remember when he skipped summer football practice until he was guaranteed more free periods?…Liked to put his money where his nose is…"Whaddya mean? The only substance I might ever abuse is you!" (Sorry, big guy! Just kidding)
Football 1,2,3,4; Golf 1,2,3,4

DONALD TRUMP

"I am the greatest."—Muhammad Ali

"Stinky"…"Oh, man, it's unfuckingbelievable"…Trophy fixation…Thanks for bankrupting the Junior Achievement program, dork…Eyes popped when a certain longstanding relationship with a certain *top* foreign-exchange student collapsed, thanks to a certain freshman girl…"In terms of quality"…Loves: watching the tube with some imported brews and a special lady…Goal: to have a different waterproof tie for every day of the month
ROTC 1,2; Football 1,2 (equipment manager); Junior Achievement 2,3,4

IVANA TRUMP

"One less egg to fry."—Bacharach & David

"The Shelf"…"S'ever Exy"…"Pssssst"…Mysterious past…"That's her—the blond with the can of gold spray paint"…What did she see in that dink?…Memo to classmates: "Thanks you to my American friends who have support me. I am not ever forgetting you!"…Memo to DT: "Eat the defecation and be dead"…Miss Smith's favorite
JV Ski Team (captain) 1; Helping Hands 3; Prom Committee 3,4

ROBERT EDWARD TURNER

"We had joy, We had fun, We had seasons in the sun."—Terry Jacks

"Terrible Ted"…"It's admirable to say what you think, Mr. Turner. Just think it first"…Current-events buff…Lose the skipper's hat, dude…The Braves' hat, too…"Me Tarzan"… Is he feeling the burn, or what? (Work it! Work it, JF!)…Ambition: party hearty—and get respect
A/V Squad 2,3,4; Love the Planet Society 4

BARBARA WALTERS

"I was gratified to be able to answer promptly, and I did. I said I didn't know."—Mark Twain

"Babs"…No, it's not a joke, that really is the way she talks (ouch!)…"But I'm a serious person!"…*Weally!*…Used dad's connections to get into A/V Squad…"Nice people don't gossip—they spread news"
The Mercury 1; Cinephiles 2,3,4; Slimnastics 4; Prom Committee 4

ANDREW LLOYD WEBBER

"Take a letter, Maria, address it to my wife. Say I won't be coming home, gonna start a new life."—R.B. Greaves

"Beaver Lips"…Just add Rice (only kidding!)…Tone it down a little, why dontcha!… How'd he get his breakups announced over the PA system?
Band 1; Thespian Society 1,2,3,4

GEORGE WILL

"Do ya think I'm sexy?"—Rod Stewart

"Poindexter"…"Is that a clip-on?"…Brags that he's memorized Bartlett's…Regrets: calling Principal Bush "a lapdog"…Treasures: all that fascinating time on the bench
Ping-Pong Club 1; National Honor Society 1,2,3,4; The Mercury 1,2,3,4; A/V Squad 3,4; Baseball 4 (equipment manager)

OPRAH WINFREY

Thanks, Spiels, for believing in me.

"It's HARPO backwards!"…"Tell me about it"…Guidance Department intern… Ann-Margret? You must be joking!…Control freak much?
A/V Squad 2,3,4; Slimnastics 3; Cinephiles 3

THOMAS K. WOLFE

"Just know your lines and don't walk into the furniture."—Spencer Tracy

"Balzac"…"You write nicely, Mr. Wolfe, but didn't anybody ever teach you punctuation?"…The instant expert…For a fairly cool guy, he sure dresses like a nerd…Always bragging about riding the subway to school…"No, try it my way"…Loves: the spats he stole from the band supply room
National Honor Society 1,2,3,4; The Mercury 1; Calliope 2,3,4; Junior Toastmasters 3,4

MORTIMER ZUCKERMAN

"I've got to find my corner of the sky."—from *Pippin*

"Morty"…Has never dated the same girl three Saturday nights in a row …What does he *do* on the newspaper? Well, can we say "Bought The Layout Boards" on the masthead?…Law school next?…Go ahead, butter him up. Flattery will get you everywhere…Ambition: to employ everyone he knows
JV Wrestling 1; Student Council 2,3,4; The Mercury 3,4; Calliope 3,4; Baseball 2,3,4 (captain); Prom Committee 4

Lose a bet, Sylvester? Stallone with his prom date, the Science Department's Mrs. Schroeder.

Senior Prom

**1991 Prom Theme:
"NOTHING COMPARES 2 US"**

▲ Junior Grace Jones brought a certain special *je ne sais quois* to her duties as decorations assistant, no?

▲ Sandra Bernhard and date? (Just kidding!)

► What's with Al D'Amato's super-excited date? She must've owed him a favor. (Just kidding!)

▲ *"And another thing—who made the decision to give the refreshments-booth contract to 'Stinky' Trump?"*

◄ No high school punks for her! Resourceful Joey Heatherton brought a man who described himself as a Japanese tycoon.

Mr. Schwarzenegger came to the prom accompanied by a friend he introduced as Miss Vavoom.

"Hey, bud, move along if you don't got your ticket ready." Many thanks are in order to Don "Stinky" Trump, who filled in for class treasurer Mike Milken at the last minute as prom comptroller.

"If she don't pay, she don't get in the door." Stinky made a dandy ticket taker!

"Who dropped a rose?" Barbara Walters's date, Merv Adelson, can't believe he's at the prom with a gal in a bathrobe!

"Hey, aren't you the one I caught tryin' to sneak in earlier? Get lost, ya runt!"

"Hey, your hair smells great!" Senior Bob Gottlieb tries out an old, old line on a fellow promgoer.

Are the gals getting taller, or the guys getting smaller?

Saul "Porky" Steinberg and his steady, Gayfryd

Carolyne Roehm and Henry "Stumpy" Kravis

"Y'see, I wear my cowboy boots and jeans with a tux jacket!" Ralph Lauren explains his personal promwear philosophy to enchanted onlookers.

Tina Brown (getting her foot crunched) and Harry Evans

Senior Prom

Giddiest: Bill Buckley (not, we notice, dancing with his date, Pat)

Dance Fever!
They could have danced all night, but their drivers' shifts ended at 2:00 a.m.

Most Inventive: Steve "Dancing Machine" Ross, who played a mean air guitar as well as air maracas!

Most Partners: Morty Zuckerman, whose personal assistant was assigned the task of filling his dance card months in advance.

..."Are you sure she's next?"

Most Unembarrassed Doing the Bump: Gloria "Bunny" Steinem

Prom Queen

Don't worry, girls, it's only a popularity contest, based almost entirely on your physical appearance! Left to right: Susan Sontag—eyes closed with the thrill of the moment; Gloria "Bunny" Steinem, who changed into a more feminine outfit for the judging; Prom Committee member Georgette Mosbacher; Sandra "Tiger" Bernhard; top Czechoslovakian exchange student Ivana Trump; Sydney Biddle Barrows, who came without a date because she had fixed up all the boys with other girls; Cherilyn Sarkasian; Prom Committee member Shirley "Wench" Lord.

Hey, Madonna, don't be a sore loser!...

The Prom Queen Herself, Miss Spy High

...though it'd be hard to be any sorer than Don "Stinky" Trump, who took Ivana's coronation pretty hard. Seems he forgot that his date, Marla, being only a freshman (albeit an extremely popular freshman), wasn't eligible to compete.

Ivana Trump, who, through tears of gratitude, thanked her surgeon, Dr. Steven Hoefflin, and told classmates, "Never I will be forgetting the old, good days or the tiny people."

51

Student Council Also-Rans

Not everyone can be a winner. All the candidates tried hard, but some just weren't popular enough to hold class office.

Bill Cosby's unsuccessful bid for treasurer turned on the slogan "Pudding Pops in Every Vending Machine."

Senior Carl Bernstein ran unsuccessfully for class president: "Words fail me. I forget what I was going to say. Never mind..." Nice *platform*!

Donny Trump for president? No way—even though he offered $1.50 in roulette chips to anyone who voted for him.

Nora Ephron tried for VP: "I demand that you stop laughing at me!" (Especially you, Carl.)

Hey, Dave, we know you take your ethnomusicographic studies seriously, but this is America, and in America we wear shoes!

"Where are the fries with gravy and the double chocolate Slim-Fast?" Senior Mike Nichols and his brainiac sidekick, sophomore Carrie Fisher, midway through their regular Wednesday-afternoon Eat-Everything-on-the-Menu-athon at the malt shop.

SENIOR LIFE

A poignant moment: waiting in line to be fitted for his cap and gown, senior Bobby DeNiro contemplates all his happy, happy times at SPY High.

A little smoky in there for you, Rupert?

SENiOR LiFE

Anything for chicks in leotards, right? Dedicated senior Carl Bernstein sits through "Amazing Grace" for the third time at the campus coffeehouse.

Grrrr! What a tough guy! (Note to readers: senior Julian Schnabel paid us to include this photo. *Just kidding!*)

"Sheesh!" The life of a guidance counselor in a nutshell.

"I know it's called the Brotherhood Luncheon, but why aren't there any chicks at my table?" Donald "Stinky" Trump seems to be having a thought as he sits between Cooking teacher Mr. King and fellow senior Jesse Jackson.

To Student Council representative Bill Bradley, even the opinions of the lowliest freshman are important. Here, frosh Paul Simon complains about a bunch of bigger kids that keep calling him Wiggy.

Mr. Lewis, the Food Services manager, hugs his protégée senior Sylvia "Steam Tray" Miles.

Don't Jane Pauley's gums ever dry out?

Nurse Westheimer always has time for her "kids." Here she reassures senior exchange student Ivana Trump about the long-term side effects of surgery.

▲ Senior George Will has resorted to taking freshmen on dates—they're the only ones who haven't heard that he ▼ always brings a book! No score!

A GIRL'S SECOND-BEST FRIEND Top exchange student Ivana Trump poses with her poodle Taffy, who provided the inspiration for her hairdo.

SENIOR LIFE

"Show me how to make a clean right cross, and then I'll be a really famous writer." Seniors Jay McInerney and Norman Mailer horsing around again!

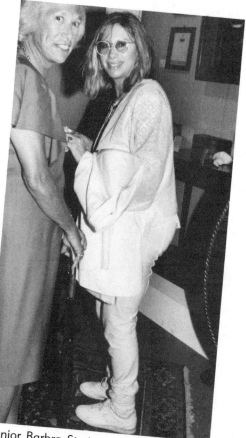

Senior Barbra Streisand, here on a field trip to a local antiques dealer, has always been known for her great taste in guys and her fabulous knack for casual sweat-shirt dressing.

ACTIVITIES

Caution: (Make-Out) Artists at Work (Just Kidding!)

the ART CLUB

From prehistoric cave paintings to giant paintings of soup cans, art has always come from man's most intense desires and fears. And membership in the Art Club has always come from man's intense desire to make girls think he's sensitive (just kidding, guys!). Also, the possibility of selling the stuff.

Senior Sylvester Stallone signs his highly controversial and socially relevant painting "GODDES$ (handprint) (handprint) SANTA GO."

Hey, come on, turn around—I'm not finished yet! Junior LeRoy Neiman, one of our most prolific artists, fulfills an assignment for Life Drawing class, sketching a couple of seniors lounging in the cafeteria. Why just Jack and Warren? Ask LeRoy.

Outspoken sophomore graffiti artist Corbin Bernsen completing a socially relevant work he calls "JoHaNNeSBuRG HiGH SCHooL" ▼

Those Who Can, Do; Those Who Can't... Senior Henry Kravis became the first Art Club member in history who never attempted to produce any art. "Stumpy" says, *Why make it if you can buy it?*

Sophomore Whoopi Goldberg with her sculpture called "A Rolling Stone Gathers No Moss, but If You Put Elmer's Glue on Your Shoes, Stuff'll Stick"

Senior Warren Beatty puts the finishing touches on a large artwork in cement entitled "My Name."

Ars Longa, Vita Brevis, Publicitas Longissima!

Self-portraits were all the rage this year.

"Bob to the Fourth Power," by junior Bob Colacello

Senior Gordon "Stinger" Sumner with his sculpture "My Reproductive Organ"

Built for Comfort, Not for Speed Sylvester makes himself at home in a chair construction called "Sit on It," an homage to senior Oprah Winfrey.

Pictures in an Exhibition: The Spring Art 'n' Stuff Show

Senior Norman Mailer—that's iced tea he's guzzling, we're absolutely positive—gooses sophomore Norris Church in front of her paintings "Bogie" and "Stoogie."

Freshman Allan Carr, clowning in front of another Church painting, "Evil Old Closet Case on the Horn"

An unsigned sketch of ROTC adviser Mrs. Helmsley ➤

59

Band

◄ Once again, ever-changing senior Michael Jackson was appointed Drum Major—and it wasn't just because he owns the suit! He's really talented, for a white guy, and the crowds love it when he does that funny walk!

It takes a great deal of skill and concentration to walk in a straight line and blow hard at the same time.

▲ BLAT! Always there when you need him, Driver's Ed teacher Mr. Dukakis filled in for a trumpet soloist who had a few too many frozen Margaritas before halftime. And once he mastered the spit valve, he played like a real pro!

Chorus

Orchestra

Maestro? Donny Trump contributed to the fund drive to pay for the orchestra's special concert trip to Phoenix—but only if they let him conduct!

The Impossible Dream. Students Bruce Springsteen, Bob Dylan and Mick Jagger lead the Boys' Chorus in a medley of songs from *Man of La Mancha*.

"Music hath charms to soothe the savage breast"—and that, we hope, means Erica's! The co-presidents of Girls' Chorus, juniors Judy Collins and Erica Jong, perform an a cappella rendition of Aerosmith's "Janie's Got a Gun."

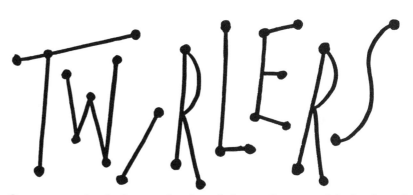

TWIRLERS

Sure, everybody loves the band, but what would the band be without the Twirlers, those muscular (in all the right places!) gals whose skills with a baton and a set of spangles never cease to amaze? This year, the Twirlers were the recipients of a generous donation from senior Drum Major Michael Jackson, who funded a whole closetful of new Twirler costumes.

▲
Superskinny senior Twirler Joey Heatherton looks like she was born in her after-hours Twirler caftan, suitable for bonfire pep rallies, parent-teacher conferences or après-school hot chocolate.

Superbusy junior Twirler Nikki Haskell, photographed at the prom with Drum Major Michael Jackson, shows off a fur-trimmed Twirler outfit suitable for formal occasions. ▲

Supersmiley junior Twirler Anna Wintour looks smashing in her new daytime Twirler outfit, appropriate for class, morning pep rallies, or lunch with Father.

Superpopular sophomore Twirler Carrie Leigh, here with Twirler faculty adviser Mr. Hefner of the Industrial Arts Department, sports a casual Twirler costume that's best reserved for spring-break pep rallies in Florida and for Twirler fundraising exhibitions. ▲

HEAVE HO! Twirler boys Emilio Estevez and Charlie Sheen hoist their spangled cargo—junior Twirler Jo Anne Worley—towards the opposing school's locker room! Sis boom baaaah!

Senior Sandra Bernhard was cut from the squad—adviser Hefner said that twirling a baton with your eyes closed is against the school board's safety code.

THESPIAN
★★★★★★★★★★★★★★★★
SOCIETY

Estragon: "He said he'd come."

Vladimir: "He said he'd come."

Waiting for Godot, by Samuel Beckett. Directed by Thespian Society president Kevin Kline.

Vladimir ....Mortimer Zuckerman
Estragon......................Gordon Sumner
Pozzo ....Si Newhouse
Lucky ....Robert Gottlieb

A Doll's House, by Henrik Ibsen. Directed by Thespian Society president Kevin Kline.

Nora ....Kathleen Turner
Torvald ....Judd Nelson

"You're insane! You've no right! I forbid you!" Junior Kathleen Turner as Nora gets her cue from the stage manager, junior Dawn Steel, before taking the stage.

Life Situations Involving Fame

Some members of the audience were especially riveted by the production number "Matchmaker"!

Director Kline offers some advice to freshman Phoebe Cates after rehearsal.

Fiddler on the Roof, by Joseph Stein, Jerry Bock and Sheldon Harnick. Directed by Thespian Society president Kevin Kline.

Tevye ....Judd Nelson
Golde..............................Barbra Streisand
Daughters.........................Cher Sarkasian, Madonna Ciccone and Phoebe Cates
Yenta the Matchmaker ....Fran Lebowitz

"Who are you?" said Alice.

Alice in Wonderland, by Lewis Carroll. Directed by Thespian Society president Kevin Kline.

Alice ....Meryl Streep
The Duchess ....Sydney Biddle Barrows
The Caterpillar....................Michael Eisner
The Mad Hatter ....Judd Nelson
Tree.................................Mary McFadden
Flower...........................Gayfryd Steinberg
Flower ....Anne Bass

(The Tree...

...and the Flowers had no lines but sure looked super!)

"Tut tut, child. Everything's got a moral if only you can find it!" quipped the Duchess.

Lysistrata, by Aristophanes. Directed by Thespian Society president Kevin Kline.

Lysistrata ....Sigourney Weaver
Cinesias ....Bruce Springsteen

"Can't live with them, or without them. Hunh!", says Cinesias.

Director Kline explains to sophomore Sigourney Weaver that while tragedy *breaks*, comedy *bends*.

THESPIAN SOCIETY

◄ "STEL-LA!" Senior Julian Schnabel's Stanley was pure brute!

A Streetcar Named Desire, by Tennessee Williams. Directed by Thespian Society president Kevin Kline.

Stanley Kowalski ....Julian Schnabel
Blanche DuBois ....Shirley Lord
Stella ....Tama Janowitz
Mitch...................................Judd Nelson

"Chicks and geese and ducks better scurry!" Where've you been hiding that baritone, Norman?!

Oklahoma!, by Richard Rodgers and Oscar Hammerstein. Directed by Thespian Society president Kevin Kline.

Curly ....Norman Mailer
Laurey....................................Jane Pauley
Aunt Eller ....Oprah Winfrey
Jud Fry ....Mike Ovitz
Ado Annie...............Pat Kennedy Lawford

"Get thee to a nunnery!" Understudy Monheit as the Dane.

Sophomore Arsenio Hall warms up with some mime exercises.
◄

"But what's my motivation for gravedigging?" Freshman Jeff Goldblum during rehearsals.

Hamlet, by William Shakespeare. Directed by Thespian Society president Kevin Kline.

Hamlet.............................Gordon Sumner
Claudius ....William F. Buckley Jr.
Gertrude ....Sally Field
Ophelia ....Phoebe Cates
Horatio................................Judd Nelson
Polonius.................................Al Neuharth
Gravedigger ....Jeff Goldblum
Player King ....Arsenio Hall
Understudy.......................Walter Monheit

1991 Thespian of the Year Award

Sophomore Judd Nelson is the recipient of the Victor Mature Thespian of the Year Award. The Great Nelsoni, as his pals call him, was cited for his dedication and for his versatility.

Hey, let's not forget the obligatory shot of the less popular people who work behind the scenes! Stage manager Dawn Steel and her crew of techies: Stanley Jaffe, Tony Thomopoulis, Jeff "Sparky" Katzenberg and Ronnie Meyer.

Nelson as the Mad Hatter...   ...Torvald   ...Horatio   ...Mitch   ...and Tevye.

Future Cosmetologists of America

Miss Smith from the cafeteria, faculty adviser (yes—we know she's not *really* "faculty," but...), demonstrating the fundamentals of public lipstick application...

... while one of her most dedicated pupils, senior Shirley Lord, studies her every move.

This organization is dedicated to the proposition that good grooming is one of the foundations of our American way of life. In FCA, the focus is on human values. Hence, our Three Precepts: we believe that to look good is to do good; that beauty is more than skin-deep; and that people will like you better if you have lots of pearlized cheekbone highlighter on.

In one of the club's most popular activities, Cross-Dress-Or-Carry-a-Tiny-Dog Day, Mr. Sununu of the Math Department and senior Dan Rather are shown here flanking school secretary Miss Rivers. ▲

A basic rule: *Hair can never be fussed with enough.* Junior Dawn Steel proves this during a panel discussion in film class... ▲

...and sophomore Eric Roberts demonstrates that if your hair looks silky and manageable, no one will notice that your pants need pressing. ➤

Another axiom: *Beauty has a heart.* Because beauty is not democratically distributed, club members are encouraged to try to see the world through others' eyes. Here, sophomores Brooke Shields and Christie Brinkley engage in a day-long "Disfigured Like Me" experiment designed to impart some sensitivity about the lives of the Beauty-Impaired.

"Piggy Banks Are for Riffraff," Say the Disgraced Business Leaders of Tomorrow

"People will try to put you down all along the way, but don't listen—chances are they're just jealous of your gold-leaf picture frames and red-flocked wallpaper," club president Saul Steinberg told assembled members.

Senior Donald Trump thinks that anyone can become rich and powerful if they follow his simple two-step plan: (1) Always surround yourself with overexercised young women with highly processed hair; and (2) Get a shiny brass nameplate for your desk that says something really important-sounding like "Mr. Big Stuff."

Man in a glass booth—with bars? (Just kidding!) After a hard day of trading stocks on inside information, Young Speculators president Mike Milken likes to unwind with a little mime.

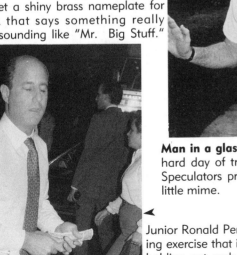

Junior Ronald Perelman participates in a confidence-building exercise that involves walking through a crowded street holding out cash with your eyes closed. The lesson: if you look like you know what you're doing, no one will ever get the better of you.

YOUNG SPECULATOR$

Helping Hands Inc.

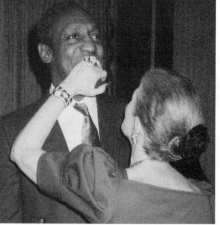

A member of the club's Community Oral Hygiene Committee brushes up on intramural flossing technique with willing volunteer Bill Cosby of the senior class.

After much coaxing, the Toys for Tots Committee finally convinced senior Donald "Stinky" Trump to part with a toy airplane.

This year's used-clothing drive for disadvantaged pets was bigger and better than ever! Sophomore Ron Reagan shows off a newly-suited-up stray...

◄

...and past PTA president Mr. James Stewart snuggles a malnourished monkey in a little ermine jacket donated by senior Gayfryd Steinberg. ▼

School nurse Mrs. Westheimer runs regular after-school workshops to teach Helping Hands members how to feed rich desserts to those less fortunate or less tall than themselves.

Ever the cheerful guinea pig, Nurse Westheimer slurps up a fingerful of frosting from feeder-trainee Robin Leach of the junior class.

Others as You Would Pay Them to Do Unto You"

As part of Helping Hands' Literacy Outreach program, junior Mel Gibson volunteered to teach basic writing skills to some West Coast neighbors with chronic learning disabilities...

...and busy senior Georgette Mosbacher donated her study hall time to teach a less fortunate, not-very-clean person to read. ◄

Helping Hands president Patricia Buckley supervises as boyfriend Bill stuffs celery with peanut butter for last winter's gala Crudites for the Homeless campaign. ▼

Helping Hands' Circus Day Brings a Smile to the Live-Entertainment-Deprived

▲ Who's that talking back to Mr. Kissinger? If the shaggy wig weren't obscuring the familiar pointy ears, you'd know it's...senior Sam Donaldson!

Big Top Couple: Czech exchange student Ivana Trump snuggles up to Don in happier times.

Circus Day's student backers, Henry "Stumpy" Kravis and Mike Milken (not yet in costume), gather in the school parking lot to rehearse their zany ten-guys-climb-out-of-a-Lamborghini act. ▲

ping Pong CLUB

bridge club

This club, popular with freshmen and other less confident students, provides a safe haven for students to work off stress with the help of a paddle and a little white ball. Here, perennial Ping-Pong Club president Bernie Goetz presides over a meeting of one.

Shhhh, they're concentrating! While opponent Warren Buffett naps midtrick, baldy Ace Greenberg, left, attempts to guide his partner's next play through telepathy.

PUBLICISTS

OF

TOMORROW

"The really super thing about this club," says faculty co-adviser Mr. Franklin, "is that it gives a kid a life preserver if his real career ends up in the toilet." Left to right: faculty co-adviser Mrs. Adams, club president Sally Kirkland, Mr. Franklin and junior Morton Downey Jr.

Please someone tell us—what do these eggheads know about girls that we don't? Left to right: senior Norman Mailer, junior John Updike, senior Woody Allen.

"It's my club, and if I can't be the only one sitting down, I refuse to be in the damn photo." Club president Bill Buckley (with clipboard) wouldn't watch the birdie, but (front row, left to right) PTA members Mrs. Pilpel and Mr. Galbraith, faculty co-adviser Mr. Kissinger, (top row) Eugene McCarthy and senior Tom Wolfe would.

Hop on, Pat! Even though he practiced his speeches over and over and spent lots of money on his campaign, club president Buckley lost in his bid for Student Council president, placing a distant third behind Mario Cuomo and Al Sharpton (remember his slogan "Al justice, Al the time"?). Too bad, Bill—we loved your furry campaign mascot!

Debate Society

Muse Visits Spy High – Especially During Party Season!

CALLIOPE

As a truly astonishing assemblage of young literary talent graced our school's hallways this year, the quarterly appearance of *Calliope*, the literary magazine, was hotly anticipated by lovers of literature and their parents. But, alas, no edition of *Calliope* was published. It seems that the entire year's printing budget was spent on a series of after-school "meetings."

Calliope officers at an after-school meeting to discuss cool venues for future after-school meetings: senior Jay McInerney (president), junior Tama Janowitz (vice president), sophomore R. Couri Hay (treasurer in charge of refreshments), freshman Bret Easton Ellis (secretary)

▲

Freshman pornographer Bret Easton Ellis examines his chin in search of a whisker. ➤

Senior-class mystery: Tell us, Tina Brown, why are all the British girls so nice to *Calliope* treasurer Si "Sweatshirt" Newhouse?

At an after-school meeting to discuss refreshments for future after-school meetings, frosh Ellis tells a hilarious and very literary joke about a chainsaw to junior Gary Fisketjon.

At an after-school meeting to discuss introducing a cover charge for future after-school meetings, sophomore class clown P. J. O'Rourke (right) boasted that his date, classmate Morgan Entrekin, had the most luxuriant head of hair in the room. Sorry, Tama!

Sophomore Roxanne Pulitzer wrote a book about musical instruments! ➤

At an after-school meeting to discuss personal publicity strategies, *Calliope* president McInerney and senior Tom Wolfe demonstrate a series of classic book-jacket-photo poses.

Junior Kitty Dukakis wrote a book about drugs!

Junior Shelley Winters wrote a work of fiction!

No *Calliope* Doesn't Mean Talented Students Aren't Writing Like Crazy!

Senior Sandra Bernhard wrote a book about beauty!

And senior Roseanne Barr wrote a book about what it's like to be a short, fat, nutty person who is disliked by much of America.

Extra! Extra! It's All the News That's Fun to Print!

the Mercury

Who, What, Where, When, and How Did You Feel? Aspiring reporter Fawn Hall of the sophomore class learns the basics of journalism: Smile nicely and store your pen cap on the top of your pen. ▼

Sophomores Donna Mills and Morgan Fairchild haven't quite learned proper camera-holding technique. Girls: you have to cover some of your face with the camera to take a good picture!

Hold It, Sweetheart, Get Me Burberry's! Circulation manager Morty Zuckerman and editorial-page editor Carl Bernstein work on Advanced Trenchcoat Skills.

Wait a Second, I Have to Turn the Page. Good notes are the lifeblood of a good story. Here, *Mercury* parties editor Jeannie Williams practices on fellow student Christopher Reeve the art of accurately writing down what a subject says, or, as journalists put it, "getting quotes." ▲

From the Halls of Spy High to the Shores of Southampton, Students Enjoy Fooling Around With Firearms

R.O.T.C.

We at SPY High are free to date and prepare for our futures, to attend dances and Tex-Mex restaurants (*Nachos!*). But while we're partying at Tex-Mex places, how many of us give any thought to the gallant men and women who serve so that we can get salt stains on our lips from too many margaritas? Of course, some students—the students who have enlisted in our school's ROTC program—not only remember those who have fallen but are preparing to join them if duty calls. Thanks, you nuts!

TEN-*hut!* Mrs. Helmsley, ROTC's supervigilant adviser, shown here with members of her special guard unit, the Leonistas. Mrs. Helmsley is credited with restoring pride to an organization that had been something of a campus joke. ▲

On the front lines for peace. Freshman Peter Sellars represents China in the Model UN. He is, in fact, the only member of the Model UN's Model Peacekeeping Forces, which fill in for the Hall Monitors when senior Curtis Sliwa is out sick. ✈

Junior Mike Tyson had to be admonished not to practice his hand-to hand combat skills with his dates. ➤

When "Through the Lips and Over the Gums, Look Out Stomach Here It Comes!" Just Won't Do

The gang's all hear, hear! Student toastmaster members Tom ("*Brrrring! Zzzzzzzing!* Here's to a most fabu-wonderful host!") Wolfe, Fran ("Thanks for inviting no small children") Lebowitz and Gene ("The whoppingest whale of a good time!") Shalit.

Jr. Toast Masters

A good toastmaster knows all the ingredients of a successful event. Club vice president Tom Wolfe demonstrates proper munchie-serving technique to fellow toastmaster Gene Shalit.

NEW AGE SOCIETY

Ommmmmm. Before really big football games, as an alternative to pep rallies, Shirley gathers club members like Bella Abzug around a large crystal and leads them in a visualization power exercise for victory.

Follow the Bouncing Ball! Club president Shirley MacLaine helps fellow students in their quest for Nirvana.

What's senior Gayfryd Steinberg visualizing? Maybe a boyfriend who stands higher than her shoulders?

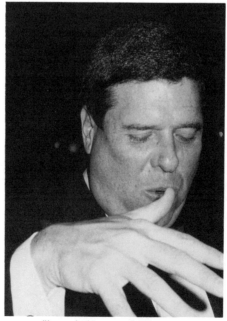

"I am light as a feather; my body is floating above the earth." Seniors Saul Steinberg and Teddy Kennedy participate in a special weight loss seminar sponsored by the New Age Society.

AUDIO squad

VISUAL incorporating cinephiles

"...Okay, now, if George starts yakking and bores everybody, I'll tug on my ear, which will be your signal to hit the lights and start the projector." From left, junior Sydney Pollack (treasurer), junior George Lucas (vice president), senior Steven Spielberg (president) and sophomore Martin Scorsese (secretary).

A/V Squad presidents past and present, including (from left to right) Steven Spielberg, Jay Stein, Sidney Sheinberg and Walter "Woody" Lantz, gather to honor Mr. Lew Wasserman, SPY High Class of 1929 (far right), in gratitude for his donation of a new slide projector for use in the large lecture room.

A/V Squad members work hard to hone their filming techniques. Here they run tape on ROTC adviser Mrs. Helmsley.

Sophomore radio buffs Howard Stern and Jessica Hahn, caught indulging in the "creative freedom" enjoyed by those who work in a medium where no one can see what you're doing.

Lights! Camera! Makeup! Junior Debbie Norville knows that understanding how all that heavy equipment works isn't everything. Here she takes a quick squat 'n' freshen-up break before going in *front* of the cameras.

The Way to a Man's Heart Is Through _Your_ Steno Pad!

Ring-a-ding-ding. Miss Sawyer of the English Department, the club's faculty adviser, shows freshman Debbie Gibson how to dial with wet nails. ◄

Look! Two-handed! ▼

TWA Coffee? Or TWA Tea? Future Flight Attendants of America, a new spin-off club of Future Administrative Assistants, is chaired by junior John Ritter with the aid of sophomore Julianne Phillips (right). ▼

◄ **Power pants suit!** Senior Georgette Mosbacher heads out to her after-school job as a receptionist at the local Chrysler dealership.

Future secretaries go places! Senior exchange student Ivana Trump finds that her new phone skills really pay off in her hectic part-time job in telemarketing.

A good secretary will never go out of style. The skills of typing, making coffee, remembering other people's wedding anniversaries, and knowing how to put toner in the copier will serve you well during those times of life when you don't have a rich spouse.

When Your Bodyguard Is Off-Duty...

These volunteers, led by senior Curtis Sliwa (left), keep our hallways safe—except, that is, when it comes to thugs attacking seniors Dan Rather and Georgette Mosbacher, to name a few.
◄

HALL MONITORS

Senior Mike Nichols is part of a volunteer undercover security force that patrols outside a canine beauty salon favored by animal-loving students. ▲

"To ward off an oncoming attacker, just throw things," says junior Sam Shepard, here flinging a down vest at members of the Shutterbug Club.

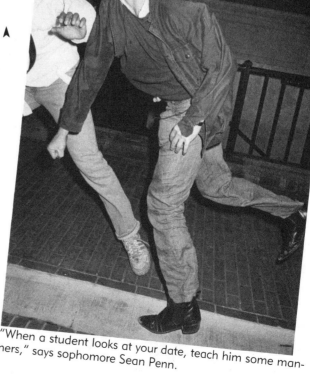

"When a student looks at your date, teach him some manners," says sophomore Sean Penn.

What's Cooking?

Too many cooks... After gagging on one of Czechoslo-vakian exchange student Ivana Trump's special Viennese pastries, sophomore Tatum O'Neal paid her cooking partner back with a few extra shakes of hot pepper on her own fettuccine Alfredo! Ah-ah-ah-*choo!*

Under the watchful eye of cooking teacher Mr. King, junior Mike Tyson pursues the perfect pancake. (Aren't Buster Douglas's a little fluffier? Ow!)

"Just keep on smiling, Barbara, and I'll stop squeezing your knuckles." Senior Barbara Walters samples one of classmate Don "Stinky" Trump's special peanut-butter-and-caviar sandwiches. ➤

Always-helpful Mr. Dukakis of the Driver's Ed Department is happy to help out in a pinch. Here he shows the "What's Cooking?" Society how to make his special fried dough, Greek style. (Note the sanitary food-preparation gloves!) ▼

Hunky soph Jean-Claude Van Damme says that al fresco Jazzercise combines two of his favorite things: kickboxing warm-up stretches, and using his Ray Bans as a dumbbell!

BURN THE BUNS! BURN THE BUNS! Senior Al Sharpton

LIMBO YOUR WAY TO A MORE LIMBER YOU! That's what school messenger Walter Monheit says. ▼

HAYUUGH! Sophomore showman Peter Allen practices a jazz-tap aerobics routine using human free-weights.

Club president Bianca Jagger must be hooked on a feeling—or something!

JAZZ ERCISE

Jazzercise Club president Bianca Jagger (center) sits with visiting lecturer Martha Graham and fellow Jazzercisers.™

Junior Mort Janklow loves the waist-whittling twist moves!

Students Celebrate Bygone Eras When There Were Better Parties Than Today

MODERN HISTORY CLUB

FEELIN' GROOVY? Meg Ryan and date Dennis Quaid came to 1960s Appreciation Day, decked out in two wildly different styles from that decade—she did Janis Joplin, while he did the Rabbit Angstrom, open-collared-Dacron-sportshirt thing.

50's
Appreciation Society

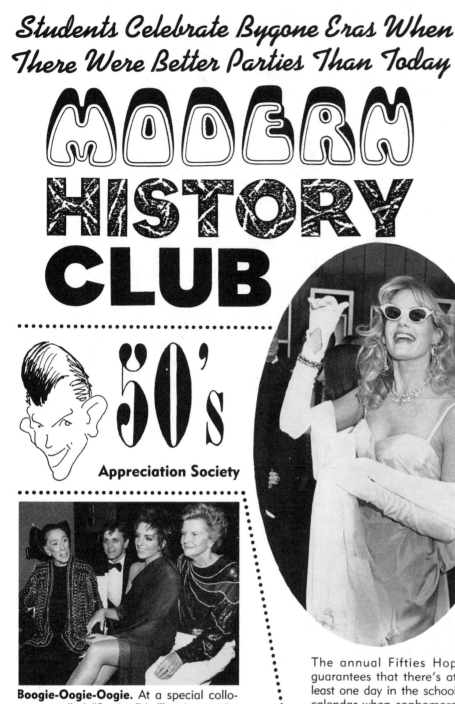

The annual Fifties Hop guarantees that there's at least one day in the school calendar when sophomore Daryl Hannah won't look goofy!

60's
Appreciation Society

Boogie-Oogie-Oogie. At a special colloquium called "Studio 54: Touchstone for a Fucked-Up Generation," guest lecturer Miss Graham beams at her protégés in Seventies Studies, juniors Mikhail Baryshnikov and Liza Minnelli, and special guest speaker Betty Ford.

Juniors Tiny Tim and Judy Carne put on fright masks to re-create the Summer of Love.

70's
Appreciation Society

Seniors Calvin Klein and Fran Lebowitz share a nostalgic moment listening to the soundtrack to *Saturday Night Fever*. ➤

Who was the swingingest chick at 1960s Appreciation Day? It was a toss-up between those two miniskirt-mad juniors Joni Evans (dig that frosted lip gloss!) with her Carnaby Street look, and Frost 'n' Tip buff Binky Urban.

82

Travel to Far-Off Lands, See Ancient Cultures, Meet Exotic Peoples, and Take Their Music!

Ethnomusicologists-R-Us

Not pictured: Paul Simon, Sandra Bernhard, John Lurie

Junior Linda Ronstadt thinks this guitar player is muy macho!

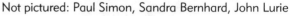

All smiles—sort of. Gordon "Stinger" Sumner, club vice president, beams with Amazonian Indian Raoni dos Metuktire, an important visitor whom Stinger spent an entire day showing off at school!

Can you find the geek in this picture? (Just kidding!) With a group of authentic visiting musicians from Brazil, club president David Byrne practices the tribal percussive technique known as clapping.

Students Demand to Know: What Are Those People Who Work for Us Really All About?

Attired in middle-class camouflage gear—stretch jeans and pigtails—junior Jerry Hall completes her fieldwork for a term paper to be called "Beyond Ban-Lon: How the Little People *Do* Matter" ▼

SOCIOLOGY CLUB

As part of a special consciousness-raising school assembly presented by the Sociology League, sophomore Brooke Shields joins friends in a skit about domestic violence.

"Adam and Eve on a raft for the broad in the hat!" By interacting with employees in an actual coffee shop, junior Bianca Jagger gathers important credits for her independent-study project.

83

Foreigners Are People Too Society

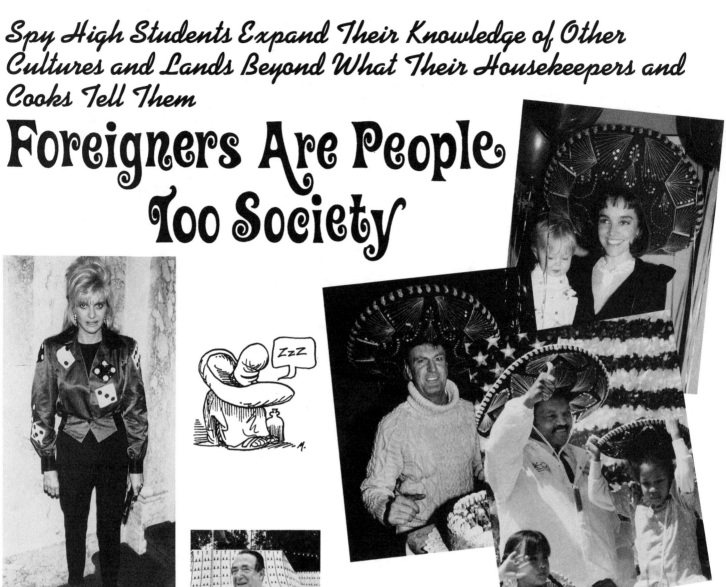

Whoops! Here's what a ▲ señorita from Czechoslovakia thinks "Dress Spanish" means. Nice one, Ivana!

▲ Three Amigos man the cake tables at November's Spanish club bake sale. Sophomores Brooke Adams and Peter Allen and senior Jesse Jackson say, "Mucho bueno!"

Junior Robert Maxwell shows some ankle at Morocco Day events.

Sophomore Cornelia Guest ▲ wearing the native costume of a Romanian prostitute for Formerly Warsaw Pact Nations Day

▼ Driver's Ed teacher Mr. Dukakis, the only person avowedly of Greek extraction at SPY High, imported family members from the Hellespont to participate in Greek Day.

84

"Rock out, people!" The audience sure put their hands together for Rob! ➤

Nice...tonsils, Marla!

"Come in, 99! I'm stuck in a large vat of nougat." ▼

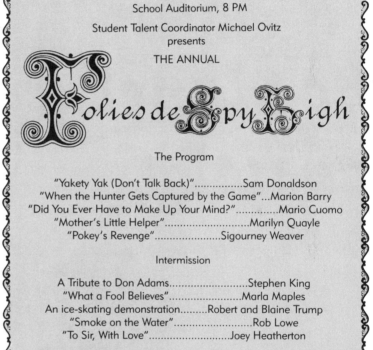

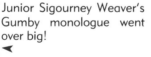

Junior Sigourney Weaver's Gumby monologue went over big! ◄

Sophomores Robert Trump and his steady, Blaine, did their marvelous "Second Bananas on Ice" routine. ➤

Joey dedicated her song to Principal Bush.

Earth Awareness Day: To Try to Become More Aware About

Earth Awareness Day ceremonies began with an address by Mr. Haig of the Social Studies Department, delivered from behind a bale of hay that was actually planted and harvested by SPY High students and their Mexican gardeners! ◄

Extremely clean freshman Johnny Depp says, "What's so bad about the Greenhouse Effect? Look how good my science project grew in the school greenhouse!" ◄

LOVE the planet society

Junior Don Johnson delivered a speech on the theme "An Apple a Day Keeps the Babes Smooching You All Over."

Spy High ♥ Veggies!

Love the Planet Society (formerly Love the Earth Society, formerly Love the Environment Society, formerly the Ecology Awareness Committee, formerly the Nature Club) members know that a lot of the world's pollution is caused by cows, through the energy expended in raising them and through their emissions. Solution: more salmon medallions and chicken paillard in the cafeteria!

▲ At a special lunch-hour assembly, junior Gloria Vanderbilt analyzed the four basic food groups and the three basic types of salad dressing.

▲ **Way to Shovel It!** Chairman of the Growin' Things Committee, sophomore Tama Janowitz

Gourd Almighty! Freshman exchange student Gloria von Thurn und Taxis reported on the value of the pumpkin as a versatile planet-minded replacement for the beanbag chair. ◄

Junior Billy Crystal earned some pocket ▲ money with just a shovel and a smile.

Mike Milken found that small animals and birds actually seem to respect him.

Unpopular senior Andrew Silverstein wearing special protective eyewear to block out harmful rays that exist in our planet's atmosphere.

Animals: More Than Just Tasty Food and Winter Coats!

In addition to giving us an excuse for getting out of class, Earth Awareness Day provided an opportunity for students to draw closer to the other living, breathing passengers on spaceship Earth.

Our undersea friends weren't forgotten, either! Junior Grace Jones took a turn as a giant mollusk and then wrote about it in a super biology paper called "Bivalved Like Me." ▶

Sophomore Cornelia Guest compared profiles with a camel. (Hey, Cornelia, doesn't its nose look just like...?) ▼

Senior Jesse Jackson tried ▲ again to convince everyone that he really is just a simple country boy.

During the part of the day reserved for developing greater empathy for endangered species, junior Mario Buatta tried to see things from the perspective of the Snub-Nosed Mallard. Beside him, senior Pat Buckley portrayed a Masked Gecko.

Students at SPY High enjoy few activities as much as slumming. And so the junior class sponsored Western Heritage Day, during which students wore the garments (many of them purchased at great cost from senior Ralph Lauren), played the music, ate the food (*Nachos!*) and spoke the lingo of the Old West. The result: a rootin'-tootin' good time!

Western Heritage day

"Howdy!" says buckaroo sophomore Tom Selleck to a pretty buckarina.

◄ Ultrapopular sophomore Christie Brinkley.

◄ Free-range senior exchange student Ivana Trump says, "I am loving wearing the tight and the fringed wardrobe of the frontierland of your America."

▲ Home-Ec ace Mario Buatta of the junior class shows that cowpokes don't have to be dirty and unkempt.

Tipsy-yi-nip-yip, get along little dogie! Cafeteria Lady Miss Smith had some trouble on her feet at the end of the night—guess she's used to having those steam tables to hold on to! ➤

"Ouch! That damn stuff's prickly!" Spunky sophomore Melanie Mayron didn't like the bales of hay that Miss Smith used to replace the cafeteria chairs on Western Heritage Day. Funny, her pal Polly Draper didn't seem to mind! ➤

Howdy, four-eyes! Sophmore Donna Karan won the prize for "Most Fringe Worn."

➤
Squares dance. With no television or screenings, people in the Old West had to devise their own forms of entertainment. Here spunky junior bookworm Harold Evans jauntily do-si-dos toward classmate Rex Reed.

In a moving tribute to Native Americans, senior Marilyn Quayle wears a tepee hat she designed herself.

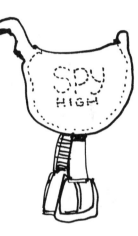

Pioneers in the Wild West liked to wear elaborate headgear made from or decorated with feathers or fur. Here popular junior Loni Anderson wears a hat festooned with eagle feathers, while junior Burt Reynolds wears a headpiece festooned with strands of human hair.

Rhinestoned Cowboys. The day ended with an old-fashioned hoedown, complete with traditional cowboy favorites. Students Peter Gabriel, Joan Baez, Bono Hewson, Tracy Chapman, Gordon "Stinger" Sumner and Bruce Springsteen join together for a rendition of "Theme Song from *Bonanza*" (*Dum da da dum, da da dum, da da dum, Bonanza!*).

Escape! Some, like Jane Fonda, came by bus....

⋀ ...Some, like Ralph and Ricky Lauren and their dog, came by Mercedes...

◄ ...but everybody made it into the pool. Of course, not everybody made it into the deep end. Here, Stumpy Kravis stalks the shallow side....

...and Eddie Murphy floats on the surface (don't tell us ▾ he's *reading*!)

the annual SPRING PICNIC

Junior Carolyne Roehm and senior Gayfryd Steinberg: *Come on*, girls, in synchronized swimming, *both* partners are supposed to raise their legs out of the water!

90

Valuable Connections in a Relaxed Setting Were at the Top of Everyone's Assignment Sheet This Day!

◄ No shortage of dog-eaters, eh, Chevy?

◄ READY, SET, SPIT! During the watermelon-seed-spitting contest, senior Dave Letterman expectorated for all he was worth...

◄ ...but the crowd was stunned by the virtuoso performance of Mike Ovitz, shown here just before launching his winning pod.

Heads up! When Mr. Schwarzenegger plays touch football, he means business!

► **Competition!** Juniors Bob Colacello and Jann Wenner flank classmate Bianca Jagger as they practice for the four-legged race. Victory, alas, was claimed by the Sandra-Madonna-Warren trio, who coasted in after...

⋀ ...the Barry Diller–Fran Lebowitz–Kelly Klein team toppled into a ditch, sending all three to the nurse's office.

◄ Freshman cutup Charlie Sheen: "This is how Mr. Forbes would have wanted to be remembered—leather, choppers, kids having fun."

Freshman Judd Nelson arrived with a chick: "I never had him in class, but anybody who'd ride a bike in a tux is okay in my book."

CYCLE CLUB

The untimely death last year of Mr. Forbes, the beloved chairman of the Social Studies Department, faculty adviser of the SPY High Cycle Club, and a really cool guy in his own right, tore a huge, gaping hole in our bosoms. To commemorate what he meant to all of us, the Cycle Club organized a special Leather Day, which proved to be one of the most popular special events on the school calendar.

Mr. Forbes, 1919-1990

We Hardly Knew Ye, Man.

Even Andy Silverstein showed up: "I never had him in class. I don't think I even knew who the fuck he was."

Howard "That's No Wig—That's My Real Hair" Stern covered the festivities for the A/V Squad: "I never had Mr. Forbes in class, but he seemed like a real freaky dude." ◄

► Senior Sylvester Stallone summed up the day perfectly: "This was so much fun, I think to myself, 'Yo! Somebody on the faculty should die *every* year!'"

◄ Very...*popular* junior Sally Kirkland combines two hobbies: cycling and weightlifting. (*Hey, Sal—why'd ya take off your jacket?*)

Not pictured: Barry Diller, Jay Leno, Michael Korda, Jann Wenner, Elizabeth Taylor

SPORTS

Front Row: A. Sharpton, W. Beatty, B. Hume, M. Kondracke, A. Hunt, J. Montana (captain), D. Quaid, W. Cosby, B. Reynolds, D. Wilder, J. Jackson, M. Jackson, B. Jackson, B. Gumbel

Row Two: Principal Bush, Coach Haig (offense), Coach Trillin (line), Coach King (backfield), Coach Tisch (linebackers), Coach Schwarzenegger (strength), Coach Berry (conditioning), Coach Sununu (film), Head Coach Mason, Coach Kissinger (defense), Coach Melman (special teams), Coach Safire (rhetoric), Coach Dinkins (uniforms), Coach Plimpton (etiquette), Coach Alda (sensitivity), Mr. Koch (team bus driver), Dr. Stuart Berger (team physician)

Row Three: J. Kriegel (towel boy), J. Koons, T. Cruise, S. Stallone, B. Diddley, D. Aykroyd, S. Ross, T. Selleck, F. Deford, J. Bon Jovi, W. Marsalis, N. Pearlstine, B. Poindexter, F. Rich, E. Murphy, M. Lupica, P.W. Herman (asst. towel boy)

Row Four: R. Gottlieb, J. Epstein, L. Taylor, L. Eisenberg, B. Musburger, A. Roker, T. Kennedy, P. Buchanan, S. Steinberg, S. Spielberg, J. Goodman, D. Crosby, S.Stills, G. Nash, N. Young, R. Young, J. Wyatt, E. Donihue, B. Gray, L. Chapin

Row Five: R. Crumb, J. Bronowski, E.E. Cummings, J. D. Salinger, B.B. Rebozo, B.B. King, I.M. Pei, L.L. Bean, Z.Z. Top, S.S. Minnow, P.P. Le Pew, V.V. Las Vegas

Football
Your Championship Pit Bulls

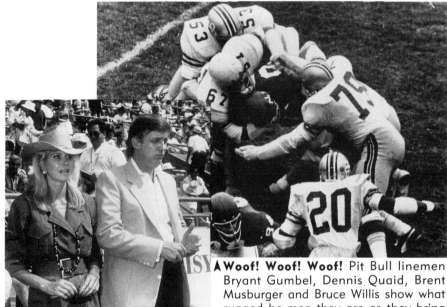

▲ **Woof! Woof! Woof!** Pit Bull linemen Bryant Gumbel, Dennis Quaid, Brent Musburger and Bruce Willis show what rugged he-men they are as they bring down junior Ethel Kennedy in a practice session.

► Third-quarter crunch time! Back when our favorite garish couple was still our favorite garish couple, Ivana stands by her man Don Trump as he counts on his fingers to calculate whether he's beaten the point spread.

During a time-out, junior Jann Wenner huddles with his close pals and classmates, Michael and Diandra Douglas, and reviews the team's options. Running play to Jackson? Screen pass to Reynolds? Long bomb to Kondracke? Or the old Statue of Liberty play with The Cos? ▼

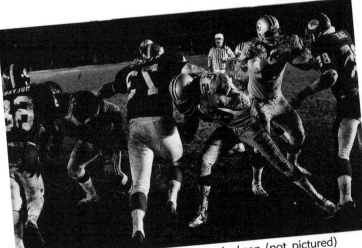

Play of the year. Halfback Jesse Jackson (not pictured) broke a scoreless tie when he took a handoff from quarterback Joe Montana (above, just a teeny bit of his helmet visible), stopped to make a brief speech, then squirted through the line for the only score of the game.

Hijinx! Football isn't only about winning or building character or making a lot of money. It's also about fun. Here Coach Alda has a good laugh after some of the fellows crammed a helmet full of Krazy Glue onto his head.

Tony Dorsett gets that old Pit Bull instinct fired up before the big game with the timeworn practice of eating a football.

Very Special Pit Bulls

Senior tackle Steve Ross was elected Most Courageous Athlete after coming back from an injury in which his head and neck were compressed into his sternum.

Senior Joe Montana was unanimously elected recipient of this year's MVP award, a large cut-glass cookie jar.

A pleasant surprise was freshman bench-warmer Rob Lowe, who wore hard-to-get-off cycling pants under his basketball shorts. ➤

Basketball

He's slow, can't jump, gets all blotchy in the face if he has to run a lot, and doesn't score much. But senior Mario Cuomo is a *competitor.* ▾

◄
Senior Jack Nicholson, the only guy on the basketball cheerleading squad, reluctantly allows fans to touch him before he hits the court.

◄ Pit Bull stars of tomorrow: sophomores Tim Busfield, Charles Barkley, Mike Gminski and Ken Olin.

Olin won admiration for having the hairiest armpits on the team, most evident when the coach had the basket lowered to 7 feet so that Olin, who is white, could perform a crowd-pleasing slam dunk. ➤

◄
Limbering up, "Sweet Georgia Brown" style, with junior Tom Macmillan before a big game, senior Bill Bradley showed off his regular-guy fashion sense by wearing a long-sleeved dress shirt under his uniform.

◄
Juggle much? Good old Mr. Dukakis of the Driver's Ed department was always around to help pass out the balls at practice.

Gymnastics

Husky junior Melanie Griffith and class-mate Diane Von Furstenburg practice the tandem balance-beam routine they call "She-Cats in Heat on a Tin Roof."

▲Mick Jagger of the senior class does his thing on the trampoline.

JO-EY! JO-EY! JO-EY! Senior Joey Heatherton is and always will be the Gymnastics Squad's Most Reliable Swinger!

Squad captain Roxanne Pulitzer stresses a holistic approach to gymnastics: "A healthy body is a flexible body, a flexible body is a happy body, a happy body is a popular body, and a popular body is a healthy body." Here she is giving one of her special rubdowns. ▼

Senior trampoline tyro Sandra Bernhard limbers up in the gym with some leg lifts.

Baseball
BatteRRRUP

This spring was a rebuilding season for the Pit Bull Nine, as many of Coach Dangerfield's star players from the 1989-90 championship team graduated, dropped out or were suspended for weapons violations. But an influx of exciting new talent took to the diamond in 1991, and dedicated fans of the Black and Blue certainly appreciated their give-it-all-you-got effort.

Diamonds are a girl's best friend: that's junior lalapalooza Kathleen Turner turning up the heat in the opponent's infield. And her batting wasn't too bad, either! (Just kidding!)▼

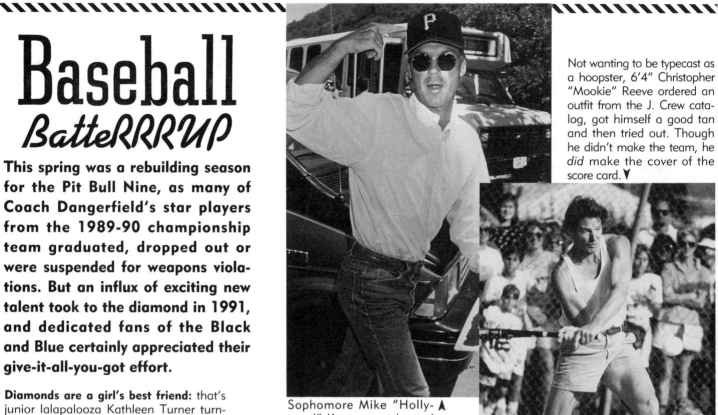

Sophomore Mike "Holly-▲ wood" Keaton was booted from the team this year for refusing to wear "that silly uniform."

Not wanting to be typecast as a hoopster, 6'4" Christopher "Mookie" Reeve ordered an outfit from the J. Crew catalog, got himself a good tan and then tried out. Though he didn't make the team, he *did* make the cover of the score card. ▼

Larry "Bam Bam" Drake showed plenty of improvement after Coach Dangerfield switched him from centerfield to bench. He wasn't allowed to play much, but after he was shown the cool way to hold a glove (index finger through the hole) Larry smiled for the fans.

Senior Mort Zuckerman is the only veteran on the squad. A seldom-used mop-up specialist during his previous two campaigns, Mort bought the team and insisted on starting every game for the Pit Bulls. ▼

Spunky sophomore second baseman Billy Crystal flashed a lot of leather in the infield. ➤

Kevin Costner's batting average improved when he took off his specs, which he'd only worn to look brainy. ◄

Don't be fooled by those vacant gazes! Sophomore Marla Hanson and senior Jay McInerney really do care who wins!

Mr. Dukakis of the Driver's Ed department, always ready to help out, threw out the first ball this season when the celebrity contracted to do it didn't show. ▼

Shortstop Paul Simon of the freshman class was a revelation in the infield. Though Paul hit an anemic .067 for the season, Coach Dangerfield notes that his tiny strike zone enabled him to lead the team in walks.

Junior Keith Hernandez suggests the SlimFast regime to Coach Dangerfield.

Cheerleading

As we all know, being popular is one of the most important things in life, and what better barometer of popularity than cheerleading try-outs? Go Team!

◄ **"2-4-6-8"** Sophomore Rosanna Arquette does an innovative bra-strap-revealing slide move.

"Who do we appreciate?" Spunky sophomore Jamie Lee Curtis really knows how to shake those pom-poms!

"Yea, Team!" Junior Faye Dunaway has her own keep-fit regimen that involves going through cheerleading practice in a black rubber sweatsuit.

"SPY High Pit Bulls!" ► Senior Joey Heatherton would've made varsity this year if she could only do those high kicks without holding her calf up with her hand. Lucky there was room for her in the Twirlers!

Beautiful Girls in Short Skirts! ////////////////////////

Junior Sally Kirkland. "Shot glass, rocks glass, martini glass, tumbler/ Come on, Pit Bulls, make him a fumbler!"

Senior Ivana Trump. "Here are we going, SPY High! Here are we going!"

Senior Madonna Ciccone. "Push 'em back! Shove 'em back!/ Hit-em-in-the-balls and then/ Tell 'em that they'll ne-ver/ Work in this town again!"

The Varsity Squad

Here they are—the *really* popular girls!

IN ACTION "Um! Ungawa! Pit Bulls got the power!"

Senior Pat Buckley: "Lean to the right/ Lean to the right/ Stand up, sit down/ Fight! Fight! Fight!"

Junior Lauren Hutton:
Give me an "F"

Junior Nikki Haskell:
Give me an "O"

Junior Sally Kirkland:
Give me an "X"

Sophomore Christie Brinkley:
Give me a "Y"

The Semaphore Foxes

Thanks to this super-elite squad of limber young ladies, reading was never so fun!

What does it spell? Yesssss! Junior Billy Joel, watching from the sidelines, still has trouble believing that he's really dating a cheerleader!
◄

◄ Practice, practice! The cheerleading squad's coach, Visiting Poet Mr. Haden-Guest, applied himself with unrelenting vim and vigor, from football season ("Swivel the arms and legs like so, love")...

...straight on through basketball season ("A periodic little nip on the leg or thigh, my dear, will keep the muscles relaxed"). ►

Spy High to Rival Teams: "Screw You If You Beat Us—We're Rich and Famous!"

◄ Freshman Ally Sheedy (in a dress she thatched herself as a Home Ec independent-study project): *What do we want?*

Pep Club

◄ Junior Tom Hayden (where was Ted when this photo was snapped?): *Victory!*

Boy cheerleaders Jon Peters and Peter Guber: *Even louder! We've got a lot of dough on this game!* ▼

Senior Donald Trump: *Say it again!*   Senior Ivana Trump: *Louder!*

SPY HIGH Refreshes!

◄ Sam Shepard, Mr. Maverick of the junior class, displays half a "Victory" sign.

Less Popular Sports

Golf

After Principal Bush, the team's coach, took a tee shot off the forehead ...

Bicycling

...the team captain, junior Dan Quayle, had to take the reins. Friends feel that Dan could have a terrific career as a golf pro ahead of him, provided he doesn't get sidetracked into some kind of desk job.

Sophomore duffer Eddie Van Halen refused to cut his hair again this year and got stuck being team caddy. ▼

Sophomores Rene Auberjonois and Ed Begley Jr., the backbone of the bicycling team, have big training plans for the summer—Ed will have to learn how to lean over the handlebars to reduce wind resistance, and Rene will be working on mounting technique.

Not-All-That-Cool Students Get a Chance to Compete, Too! \\\

Nothing comes between sophomore wrestling powerhouse Mr. T and his spandex—not even classmate and boys' cheerleading squad captain Peter Allen.
◄

HOLD THOSE TIGERS! Senior "Stumpy" Kravis... ►

...and junior Jann "I Love Being Thin!" Wenner practice their holds everywhere!

But it's Big Mike Eisner who's the real star of this scrappy team. ►

Wrestling

Looking Good! Wrestling coach Mr. Blackwell gives one of his personal protégés on the team some up-close-and-personal encouragement.

"Okay, so I'm on all fours, and now you straddle me, right?" Senior Warren Beatty went out for the Greco-Roman squad and quit after the first day of practice—when he found out that the team wasn't coed.

Tennis

What goes up... Coach Dinkins, who this year moved his office to the Tennis Center, drills his players on the fine art of watching the ball. ➤

A for effort. Junior Danny Quayle doesn't hit many, but he runs after them all.

▲**Top Lady Pit Bulls.** Freshman Steffi Graf and junior Martina Navratilova placed one-two in ladies' singles competition even though each was deep in the throes of a personal emotional crisis.

Bonk! Junior Mary McFadden demonstrates the playful "Tennis, anyone?" forehand style that drives the boys wild. ◢

Wisenheimer Morton Downey Jr. of the junior class performs the old "Wanna see a human waffle?," to the delight of his teammates. Hey Morty—nice duds!

UNDER-CLASSMEN

Student Council

Freshman Class Officers

Aw, come on, Donald! Leave the kids alone!

Jeff Goldblum, *president*
John Kennedy Jr., *vice president*
Demi Moore, *treasurer*
Rob Lowe, *secretary*
Mr. Kissinger, *faculty adviser*

Sophomore Class Officers

Spike Lee, *president*
Deborah Norville, *vice president*
Paulina Porizkova, *secretary*
Richard Darman, *treasurer*
Mr. Schwarzenegger, *faculty adviser*

Junior Class Officers

Ted Koppel, *president*
Morgan Fairchild, *vice president*
Michelle Pfeiffer, *secretary*

Billy Joel, *treasurer*
Mr. Donahue, *faculty adviser*

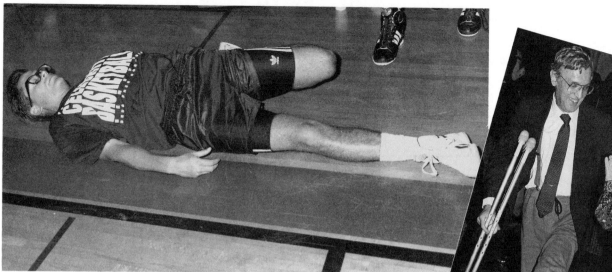

Freshman basketball player Rob Lowe tries the old *"Some-body find a candystriper, fast"* routine.

Always working! School nurse and official chaperone Mrs. Westheimer uses sign language to explain the birds and the bees to an injured underclassman between dances.

under classmen

Like most underclassmen, sophomore Martin Short affects convincing amusement any time senior Mike Ovitz deigns to speak to him.

The princess and the peabrain? Sophomore Tama Janowitz likes to study lying down on a large pile of rugs. Kooky!

Come on, Jann, ask her. It's not as if Mademoiselle Collins is going to bite you. (On second thought, don't be too sure.... Just kidding!)

Bachelors Five. After spending the early part of the evening in Kiefer's Beemer in the parking lot, freshmen Kiefer Sutherland, Emilio Estevez, Christian Slater, Alan Ruck and Jon Bon Jovi help one another stand up at the freshman mixer.

Don't worry, Linda, he'll come out sooner or later. At the Sadie Hawkins Dance, sophomore Linda Ronstadt dutifully waits outside the boys'-room door for her date.

Hey, come on now, guys! Juniors Harvey Fierstein and Richard Gere continued the age-old prank of selling "officially required" pens to naive freshmen on the first day of school.

Mr. Schwarzenegger celebrated German Reunification Day last winter by waltzing across campus. Here, prize pupil Sylvester Stallone plays along.

On registration day, freshman class vice president John Kennedy Jr. and Mrs. Schroeder of the Science Department listen excitedly to Principal Bush's welcoming remarks.

At the Sadie Hawkins Day Dance, Coach Schwarzenegger does the Pony.

It was a packed house in sophomore English Lit when student teacher Miss Sawyer lectured on *The Diaries of Anaïs Nin.*

Har har! Lovable junior Keith Hernandez holds his breath until Coach Schwarzenegger allows him and pal Rusty Staub to share a locker.

"And way out there, beyond the horizon, is a big, beautiful town called Vegas." Junior Henry Winkler talks to classmate Billy Crystal about career plans.

under classmen

Sophomore Cornelia Guest oozes the fresh-faced charm that makes her so popular with certain members of the groundskeeping staff.

Maybe if I tell her it's not my real name...? Freshman-class vice president John Kennedy Jr. wonders, halfway through the school year, how he can get ditch the sophomore "orientation guide" assigned to help him through the first week of school.

Arsenio Hall, unsuccessful candidate for junior vice president: "I want to *rule* you...."

Goldie Hawn, unsuccessful candidate for sophomore president: "If we all just hold hands and think happy thoughts..."

Sophomore Isabella Rossellini scribbles a love poem on a napkin in the cafeteria. It's called "For Dave: Meditation on a squashed squirrel."

Always-helpful Mr. Dukakis of the Driver's Ed Department agreed to take the Sociology Club on a fact-finding mission to the subway, to see how regular citizens travel to and from the places they go to earn a living. Note the subway safety gloves!

under classmen

Madonna and junior Bruce Willis were fixtures on the track this year. But who was running from whom?

Handle with care, Casey Kasem! Your junior prom date, Jean, looks like she might pop!

NOOGIES! Sophomore Peter Maas gives 'em to classmate P. J. O'Rourke.

"Four more payments and she's all mine!" Junior Leonard "Cat Litter" Stern shows off his date to the junior prom.

Juniors Danny Aykroyd and Donna Dixon. Just a nature walk, right, guys? Suuuure.

At the spring picnic, Australian exchange student Robin Leach showed SPY Highers how his mates and he dress every day Down Under.

Sophomore Donna Karan wowed her physics class with her super science project—earrings that simulate the motion of Mercury and Venus revolving around the sun.

Rules 'n' Regulations—Even for People Like Us!

STUDENT HANDBOOK, RULE 17:

Students are required at all times to maintain appropriate standards of dress. Students who violate this rule will immediately be sent home, and will not be readmitted until suitably attired.

Dean of Discipline Mr. Giuliani's Most Wanted List

...sophomore Robin Byrd ("No more than 25 percent of buttocks may be exposed")...

This year Mr. G. sent home sophomore Tina Turner ("All students must wear underwear")...

...junior Grace Jones ("No shirtless nuzzling in the hallway"—and with Rick James to boot!)...

...sophomore Nell Campbell ("*No inappropriate decolletage*")...

...junior Paloma Picasso ("*No see-through blouses on school property*")...

...sophomore Jessica Hahn ("*Exposed breasts in bondage are not permissible*")...

...senior Cher Sarkasian ("*No visible navels allowed*")...

... and freshman Martha Plimpton ("*Footwear must be worn at all times outside the locker room*").

STUDENT HANDBOOK, RULE 45:

Smoking on school property is forbidden. Violations of this rule will be punishable by a one-day suspension and the onset of various life-threatening diseases.

Mr. Giuliani's favorite pastime: spot-checking the lavatories!

SMOKING IN THE GIRLS' ROOM! Junior Anne Bass and seniors Yoko Ono and Fran Lebowitz sure are sophisticated!

AND IN THE BOYS' ROOM? Senior butt-heads Jay McInerney (with a cigarette stuck hilariously in his ear!), Jack Nicholson, Andy Silverstein, Dave "Stogie Lips" Letterman and Fran Lebowitz. Prince Nelson was also there, but he wasn't smoking. He was just, uh...watching.

Awards Assembly

Truant senior Andrew Silverstein accepts a plaque from local businesses who promised to give him something for his wall if he promised to stop hanging around in front of their establishments.

No one was surprised when junior Kathleen Turner picked up the Language Department's "At Home Abroad" scholarship, good for a semester in Europe to work on polishing fake foreign accents.

All SPY High students are VIPs but some of us are <u>V</u>VIPs

At the year-end awards assembly, junior Robin Williams tearfully accepted the Peter Pan Prize, for the student who most convincingly affects the guilelessness of youth.

Sophomores Goldie Hawn and Sally Field and senior Chevy Chase each accepted the "You Can Get There From Here" award—a prize given to students who show something called "unlikely longevity given their television beginnings."

Ombudsman Dinkins gave senior Bobby De Niro a special award, sponsored by the Student Health Services, for staying the same weight for a whole year. Way to go, Bobby!

119

Let's Go to the Cafeteria!

Tired of the same old food fights, senior Pat Buckley challenged sophomores Gilbert Gottfried and Freddie Roman to a contest of skill: canapes at ten paces. After a half dozen tosses apiece, neither had registered a bull's-eye, though Gilbert did stick one on Pat's cheek! ➤

POP QUIZ: WHO'S GOT BETTER TABLE MANNERS, BOYS OR GIRLS?

All-American sophomore Martha Stewart shovels it in!

Let them eat the cakes! Senior Ivana Trump.

Sophomore Kim Alexis sinks her teeth into a meatball. ▼

Junior Grace Jones jams in a Twinkie from the cafeteria vending machine. ▼

At the Sadie Hawkins Dance, always-ravenous senior Abe Rosenthal sucks down a quick Velveeta-on-a-Saltine while Shirley's not looking.

Senior Tom Wolfe disgorges one of Miss Smith's famous deviled eggs. ▼

▲Junior Dick Cavett loves his watercress on a bulkie!

Big John Madden of the▲ junior class—a two-fisted face-stuffer!

Sooner or later, everybody comes to the caf. Mr. Koch, our bus driver, likes to pop in for a free lunch. (Note: it may look like he's eating spare ribs, but Mr. Koch promises it's just water chestnuts.) ►

▲ Everybody's favorite Special Ed student, sophomore Mandy Patinkin, likes to help out poor old Miss Smith in the cafeteria when she's feeling low, as she seems to be here, swooning over a platter of raw meat.

◄ *Load it up and keep it coming,* junior Rex Reed seems to be saying as he moves through the line.

More, please. We pity the fool who has to tell sophomore Mr. T that there just isn't any more Diet Yoo-Hoo. ►

If you're not part of the solution... Layoffs from the cafeteria staff are a big problem. Everybody sure appreciates it when Mr. Dukakis from the Driver's Ed Department chips in. And they doubly appreciate his using medical gloves. "Germs," Mr. Dukakis has said time and again, "are bad." ►

under classmen

Can you believe that a freshman girl who wears baby-doll pajamas to dances could be so serious and knowledgeable about Central America? Neither can we! (Just kidding!)

There's junior Dan Aykroyd, ducking out the gym door after spying on cheerleading practice again! Hot in there, huh?

"You're late again, mister!" Seldom have these words meant so little so often as they have to chronically tardy junior Keith Richards.

The face of confidence. Freshman Michael J. Fox's limo driver, Evans, made sure Mike arrived good and early for his algebra final.

Always-helpful Driver's Ed teacher Mr. Dukakis was more than happy to volunteer his head when there weren't enough students to wear all the sombreros at this year's Nacho Fiesta (1991 theme: "Mexico—Land of Enchantment, Pool Attendants and Housekeepers"). ¡Olé!

Watch the Birdbrain! (Just kidding!) Homecoming Float Committee member Gayfryd Steinberg displayed an uncharacteristic bit of thrift by recycling leftover float materials into decorations for her gown!

◀ Senior homecoming Float Committee chair Ivana Trump shows the kids how homecoming floats are traditionally displayed in her native Czechoslovakia.

What with all the advances in beauty and grooming technology, competition was keener than ever this year for Homecoming Queen!

The Nervous Finalists

▲**The Candidettes:** (left to right) sophomore Suzanne Sommers; freshman Pia Zadora, who had the same hairstyle as her date, Morgan Entrekin (not pictured); freshman Carol Alt in an alluring below-the-knee wet suit; sophomore Diandra Douglas, here tugging at a pesky VPL; sophomore Blaine "The Pretty Trump" Trump; Debbie "I'm Really Smart, Really" Norville; and senior Gayfryd Steinberg.

The Winner Is...

Homecoming

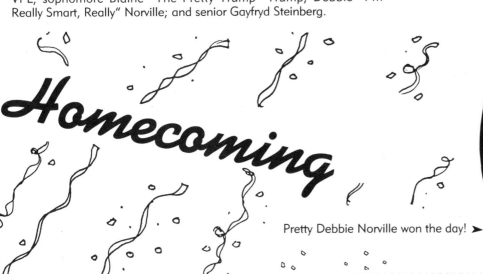

Pretty Debbie Norville won the day! ➤

Remember Your "Golden" Years at Spy High

RESTAURANT

Bellevues

"We're **Proud** of You"

– Mirabella

"Good Luck To The Class of '91"

– Hudson News

"You've Come A Long Way"

– DesignerType

"With the Compliments of…"

– Diesel Jeans

"**From your friends at…**"

– The Varsity Club

"Here's to a *Healthful*, Happy and *Productive* Future for You All"

– Marion's Continental Restaurant

"Go, You Pit Bulls! Woof! Woof! Woof!"

– Virgin Records

Virgin

"Always Remember, 'Brush after meals, and *good luck*'"

– Mark Lowenberg, DDS
& Gregg Lituchy, DDS

"Congraduations" Seniors!

– Alexander Isley Design

"Best of Luck Always"

J&B

Credits

Cover: Styled by Elissa Schappell. Quayle's shirt and shoes; Murphy's jacket and shoes courtesy of Paragon Sports.Gene Shaw/Star File (Trump); Ron Galella, Ltd. (Barr); Eve Sereny/Sygma (Allen); Anthony Savignano/Galella, Ltd. (Madonna); Larry Williams/Outline (Murphy); Mitchell Levy/Globe Photos (Pauley); R. Maiman/Sygma (Quayle). Background photo by Harris Welles.
Page 1: Pit Bull logo by Doug Taylor.
Pages 2,3: Frederic Lewis (school).
Page 7: AP/Wide World Photos (Bush).
Page 8: Smeal/Galella, Ltd. (Hall, Alonso); AP/Wide World Photos (Dinkins).
Page 9: Courtesy of Press Office President of Austria (Schwarzenegger); all others Marina Garnier.
Page 10: Scott Downie/Celebrity Photo (Lloyd); Savignano/Galella, Ltd. (Joel); Robin Platzer (Chase).
Page 11: Patrick McMullan.
Page 12: AP/Wide World Photos (Bush, Powell); Aubrey Reuben/London Features Intl. (Dinkins); Sygma (Bush and pig); all others Marina Garnier.
Page 13: AP/Wide World Photos (Liman, Giuliani); Marina Garnier (Streep); Brian Hamill (Alda); Smeal/Galella, Ltd. (Donahue).
Page 14: Marina Garnier (Helmsley, Tisch); Ron Galella, Ltd. (Sawyer); all others AP/Wide World Photos.
Page 15: Alberto Tolot (Henley); Smeal/Galella, Ltd. (Scott); all others AP/Wide World Photos.
Page 16: Marina Garnier (Plimpton, Ellerbee); Kelly Wise (Lish); Aubrey Reuben/London Features Intl. (Sawyer); NYT Pictures (Shawn); AP/Wide World Photos (Papp); Chase Roe (Franklin); all others Patrick McMullan.
Page 17: AP/Wide World Photos (Helms); M. Abramson/Sygma (Castelli); Marina Garnier (Kravis, Gottlieb); Nick Sangiamo (Sondheim); Ketner (Berry).
Page 18: Kelly Jordan/Galella, Ltd. (Collins); Marina Garnier (Gabor, Kempton); Smeal/Galella, Ltd. (Collins with Hamilton); AP/Wide World Photos (O'Connor).
Page 19: AP/Wide World Photos (Thatcher); Smeal/Galella, Ltd. (Schwarzenegger); Aubrey Reuben/London Features Intl. (Mason); Belfiglio/Galella, Ltd. (Steinbrenner).
Page 20: Dennis Brack/Black Star (Safire); Chase Roe (Moynihan); Ron Galella, Ltd. (Kissinger); Marina Garnier (Peters, Redgrave, Kirkpatrick).
Page 21: Ron Galella, Ltd. (Goldstein); AP/Wide World Photos (Gingrich); Marina Garnier (Browns, King).
Page 22: AP/Wide World Photos (Dukakis); Ron Galella, Ltd. (Selleck); Smeal/Galella, Ltd. (Davis); Marina Garnier (Schwarzenegger).
Page 23: AP/Wide World Photos (Dukakis); Ron Galella, Ltd. (Kravis); all others Marina Garnier.
Page 24: Ron Galella, Ltd. (Smith); Smeal/Galella, Ltd. (Koch); Bauer/Galella, Ltd. (Lewis); AP/Wide World Photos (List); Bob Evans/LGI (Smith with hammer).
Page 26: Marina Garnier (Cuomo, Zuckerman, Smith; Bradley); Smeal/Galella, Ltd. (top Pauley); Aubrey Reuben/London Features Intl. (Milken, bottom Pauley). Illustrations, this page and pages 27-29 by Tom Gammill.
Page 27: Smeal/Galella, Ltd. (Nicholson, Fonda); Marina Garnier (Ovitz, Turner, Klein); Aubrey Reuben/London Features Intl. (Brown, Trump); Ron Galella, Ltd. (Mosbacher, King); Savignano/Galella, Ltd. (Allen).
Page 28: Marina Garnier (Sontag, Madonna, D'Amato, McInerney, Miles); Ron Galella, Ltd. (Beatty, Walters, Jagger); Savignano/Galella, Ltd. (Cosby).
Page 29: AP/Wide World Photos (Quayle); Ron Galella, Ltd. (Madonna, Streisand, Chers); Bauer/Galella, Ltd. (Steinberg); Savignano/Galella, Ltd. (Trump); Marina Garnier (Zuckerman); Aubrey Reuben/London Features Intl. (Sting); Victor Malafronte/Celebrity Photo (Ono).
Page 30: Marina Garnier (Allen, Barrows); Ron Galella, Ltd. (Barr, Beatty).
Page 31: Smeal/Galella, Ltd. (Barr); all others Marina Garnier
Page 32: Marina Garnier (Buckley Jr.); Ron Wolfson/London Features Intl. (Byrne); AP/Wide World Photos (Canseco); Patrick McMullan (Chase); Lorraine Day (Madonna).
Page 33: Marina Garnier (Diller, D'Amato, Cuomo).
Page 34: AP/Wide World Photos (Donaldson, Farrakhan); Ron Galella, Ltd. (Ephron); Brent Petersen/ABC News (Sawyer).
Page 35: AP/Wide World Photos (Gumbel); Marina Garnier (Gottlieb, Gotti); Patrick McMullan (Heatherton).
Page 36: Sam Emerson (Jackson); Marina Garnier (Jesse Jackson, Kennedy); Ron Galella, Ltd. (King); Savignano/Galella, Ltd. (Jagger).
Page 37: Marina Garnier (Klein, Kline, Lauren, Lebowitz); Bauer/Galella, Ltd. (Kravis).
Page 38: Marina Garnier (Lord); Ron Galella, Ltd. (Mailer); Tammie Arroyo/Galella, Ltd. (MacLaine).
Page 39: Marina Garnier (McInerney, Miles); AP/Wide World Photos (Milken); Albert Ortega/Galella, Ltd. (Fonda).
Page 40: Marina Garnier (Mosbacher, Murdoch); Jeff Katz (Prince); Cardone/Galella, Ltd. (Murray).
Page 41: Ron Galella, Ltd. (Nichols, Nicholson, Ono, Clay); Marina Garnier (Newhouse, Onassis).
Page 42: Smeal/Galella, Ltd. (Ovitz, Jackson); Ron Galella, Ltd. (Pauley); AP/Wide World Photos (Quayle).
Page 43: Rose Hartman (Rosenthal); Marina Garnier (Schnabel, Ross); AP/Wide World Photos (Sharpton); Bauer/Galella, Ltd. (Cher).
Page 44: Marina Garnier (Sliwa, Steinberg); Patrick McMullan (Sontag); Smeal/Galella, Ltd. (Spielberg, Stallone).
Page 45: Marina Garnier (Steinberg, Taylor); Ron Galella, Ltd. (Sting, Steinem).
Page 46: Marina Garnier (Trumps, Turner, Walters, Webber).
Page 47: Savignano/Galella, Ltd. (Wolfe); Marina Garnier (Zuckerman, Stallone).
Page 48: Ron Galella, Ltd. (Bernhard, Donaldson); Smeal/Galella, Ltd. (Shriver); Marina Garnier (Heatherton, D'Amato); Aubrey Reuben/London Features Intl. (Jones).
Page 49: Savignano/Galella, Ltd. (Lauren); Ron Galella, Ltd. (Brown); Aubrey Reuben/London Features Intl. (Jagger); all others Marina Garnier.
Page 50: Marina Garnier.
Page 51: Ron Galella, Ltd. (Cher); Savignano/Galella, Ltd. (Ivana Trump, Barrows); Smeal/Galella, Ltd. (Bernhard); all others Marina Garnier.
Page 52: Marina Garnier (Bernstein, Trump).
Page 53: Theo Westenberger (Byrne); Marina Garnier (Fisher); Aubrey Reuben/London Features Intl. (De Niro).
Page 54: Marina Garnier (Murdoch, Schnabel, Trump); Ron Galella, Ltd. (Alda); Aubrey Reuben/London Features Intl. (Bernstein).
Page 55: Star File (Simon); Smeal/Galella, Ltd. (Pauley); Marina Garnier (Trump); Patrick McMullan (Lewis).
Page 56: Marina Garnier (Will, Streisand); Ron Galella, Ltd. (McInerney); Bettina Cirone (Trump).
Page 57: Savignano/Galella, Ltd.
Page 58: Scott Downie/Celebrity Photo (Stallone, Bernsen); Savignano/Galella, Ltd. (Kravis); Ron Galella, Ltd. (Beatty); Marina Garnier (Neiman).
Page 59: Ron Galella, Ltd. (Beatty, Sting, Colacello); AP/Wide World Photos (Helmsley).
Page 60: Smeal/Galella, Ld. (Jackson); Aubrey Reuben/London Features Intl. (Dukakis); Ron Galella, Ltd. (Jagger); Marina Garnier (Jong, Trump).
Page 61: Aubrey Reuben/London Features Intl. (Worley); Smeal/Galella, Ltd. (Hefner); Savignano/Galella, Ltd. (Bernhard); Chase Roe (Heatherton); Marina Garnier (Haskell, Wintour).
Page 62: Marina Garnier (Zuckerman); Bauer/Galella, Ltd. (Sting).
Page 63: Ron Galella, Ltd. (Barrows); Bauer/Galella, Ltd. (Streep); all others Marina Garnier.
Page 64: Jaqueline Schnabel (Schnabel); A. Gallo/Shooting Star (Springsteen); Marina Garnier (Kline, Mailer).
Page 65: Smeal/Galella, Ltd. (Hall); Savignano/Galella, Ltd. (Nelson with cap); Marina Garnier (Goldblum, rest of Nelsons).
Page 66: Marina Garnier (Smith, Lord); Patrick McMullan (Rivers).
Page 67: Aubrey Reuben/London Features Intl. (Steinberg); Ron Galella, Ltd. (Milken); Marina Garnier (Perelman).
Page 68: Aubrey Reuben/London Features Intl. (Cosby); Albert Ferreira/DMI (Trump); Smeal/Galella, Ltd. (Reagan); Bauer/Galella, Ltd. (Dr. Ruth on right); Marina Garnier (Dr. Ruth on left).
Page 69: Ron Galella, Ltd. (Mosbacher); Smeal/Galella, Ltd. (Milken); Savignano/Galella, Ltd. (Kissinger); Marina Garnier (Buckley); Patrick McMullan (Trump).
Page 70: AP/Wide World Photos (Goetz); Marina Garnier (Buffett, Downey Jr.).
Page 71: Ron Galella, Ltd. (Buckley); Marina Garnier (Allen, Wolfe).
Page 72: Patrick McMullan (Janowitz); Bauer/Galella, Ltd. (Brown); all others Marina Garnier.
Page 73: Rose Hartman (McInerney); AP/Wide World Photos (Wolfe); Savignano/Galella, Ltd. (Barr); Greg De Guire/Celebrity Photo (Winters); Ron Galella, Ltd. (Bernhard); Smeal/Galella, Ltd.. (Dukakis); Marina Garnier (Pulitzer).
Page 74: Victor Malafronte/Celebrity Photo (Mills); Smeal/Galella, Ltd. (Hall); all others Marina Garnier.
Page 75: Chase Roe (Tyson); Patrick McMullan (Sellars); Bauer/Galella, Ltd. (Helmsley); Marina Garnier (Shalit).
Page 76: Marina Garnier (Abzug, Gayfryd Steinberg); Aubrey Reuben/London Features Intl. (Kennedy, Saul Steinberg).
Page 77: AP/Wide World Photos (Helmsley); Marina Garnier (Norville); Smeal/Galella, Ltd. (Lucas); Ron Galella, Ltd. (Stern, Sheinberg).
Page 78: Theo Westenberger/Sygma (Trump); Aubrey Reuben/London Features Intl. (Sawyer); Savignano/Galella, Ltd. (Gibson); Marina Garnier (Mosbacher).
Page 79: AP/Wide World Photos (Sliwa); Savignano/Galella, Ltd. (Penn); Marina Garnier (Nichols); Betty Burke Galella/Galella, Ltd. (Shepard).
Page 80: Aubrey Reuben/London Features Intl. (Allen); John Paschal/Celebrity Photo (Van Damme); AP/Wide World Photos (Sharpton); Ron Galella, Ltd. (Jagger); all others Marina Garnier.
Page 81: Brian Quigley (Donald Trump); AP/Wide World Photos (Dukakis); Savignano/Galella, Ltd. (Tyson, O'Neal); Marina Garnier (Ivana Trump).
Page 82: Janet Gough/Celebrity Photo (Quaid); Aubrey Reuben/London Features Intl. (Carne); Ron Galella, Ltd. (Hannah); all others Marina Garnier.
Page 83: F. Stop Fitzgerald (Byrne); AP/Wide World Photos (Sting); Scott Downie/Celebrity Photo (Hope); Marina Garnier (Jagger, Hall).
Page 84: Bauer/Galella, Ltd. (Trump); Ron Galella, Ltd. (Maxwell); AP/Wide World Photos (Dukakis, Jackson); Marina Garnier (Adams, Allen, Guest).
Page 85: Bauer/Galella, Ltd. (Maples); Robin Platzer (Weaver); Ron Galella, Ltd. (King, Trump); Marina Garnier (Lowe, Heatherton).
Page 86: AP/Wide World Photos (Haig); Scott Downie/Celebrity Photo (Depp); Bauer/Galella, Ltd. (Johnson); Patrick McMullan (Janowitz); Marina Garnier (Von Thurn und Taxis, Vanderbilt).
Page 87: AP/Wide World Photos (Jackson); Smeal/Galella, Ltd. (Clay, Crystal); Savignano/Galella, Ltd. (Buatta); Marina Garnier (Jones, Guest).
Page 88: De Guire/Galella, Ltd. (Selleck); Savignano/Galella, Ltd. (Brinkley, Buatta); Scott Downie/Celebrity Photo (Mayron); Marina Garnier (Trump, Smith).
Page 89: Smeal/Galella, Ltd. (Reynolds); Savignano/Galella, Ltd. (Karan); Donna Santisi (Bono); all others Marina Garnier.
Page 90: Smeal/Galella, Ltd. (Fonda); Marina Garnier (Lauren); Ron Galella, Ltd. (Gayfryd Steinberg, Kravis); Bruce Talamon (Murphy).
Page 91: Scott Downie/Celebrity Photo (Chase); Smeal/Galella, Ltd. (Ovitz); Ron Galella, Ltd. (Klein, Letterman); Patrick McMullan (Jagger).
Page 92: Kevin Winter/DMI (Nelson); Savignano/Galella, Ltd. (Stern); Smeal/Galella, Ltd. (Clay, Sheen, Stallone, Kirkland); Marina Garnier (Forbes).
Page 93: AP/Wide World Photos (Quayle).
Page 94: Savignano/Galella, Ltd. (Wenner, Trumps).
Page 95: Bettina Cirone (Dorsett); AP/Wide World Photos (Montana); Marina Garnier (Ross).
Page 96: Capital Cities/ABC (Olin); John Paschal/Celebrity Photo (Lowe); Steve Labadassa (Dukakis); AP/Wide World Photos (Cuomo).
Page 97: Marina Garnier (Furstenburg, Pulitzer); Patrick McMullan (Heatherton); Betty Burke Galella/Ron Galella, Ltd. (Jagger); Ron Galella, Ltd. (Griffith, Bernhard).
Page 98: John Paschal/Celebrity Photo (Drake); Smeal/Galella, Ltd. (Keaton); all others Bauer/Galella, Ltd.
Page 99: Smeal/Galella, Ltd. (Costner); Savignano/Galella, Ltd. (Simon, Hansen, Hernandez); Greg De Guire/Celebrity Photo (Crystal); AP/Wide World Photos (Dukakis).
Page 100: Smeal/Galella, Ltd. (Arquette); Ron Galella, Ltd. (Dunaway, Curtis); Marina Garnier (Heatherton).
Page 101: Ron Galella, Ltd. (Buckley, Trump, Kirkland); Albert Ferreira/DMI (Madonna).
Page 102: Savignano/Galella, Ltd. (Brinkley); Ron Galella, Ltd. (Kirkland); Paul Cox (Joel); Marina Garnier (Haskell, Hutton); Patrick McMullan (Haden-Guest); John Simone (Haden-Guest dancing).
Page 103: Savignano/Galella, Ltd. (Ivana Trump); Smeal/Galella, Ltd. (Sheedy); Janet Gough/Celebrity Photo (Shepard); Marina Garnier (Trump); Scott Downie/Celebrity Photo (Hayden).
Page 104: AP/Wide World Photos (Bush, Quayle); Scott Downie/Celebrity Photo (Van Halen); Bauer/Galella, Ltd. (Begley Jr., Auberjonois).
Page 105: Ron Galella, Ltd. (Kravis, Beatty); Aubrey Reuben/London Features Intl. (Allen); Marina Garnier (Wenner).
Page 106: Bauer/Galella, Ltd. (Dinkins, McFadden); Smeal/Galella, Ltd. (Downey Jr.); Savignano/Galella, Ltd. (Graf).
Page 107: Robin Platzer
Page 108: Cardone/Galella, Ltd. (Goldblum); Patrick McMullan (Kennedy Jr.); Smeal/Galella, Ltd. (Moore); Marina Garnier (Lowe, Kissinger). Illustrations by Tom Gammill.
Page 109: Ron Galella, Ltd. (Norville, Porizkova); AP/Wide World Photos (Darman); Savignano/Galella, Ltd. (Schwarzenegger); Bauer/Galella, Ltd. (Koppel); Marina Garnier (Fairchild, Joel); Smeal/Galella, Ltd. (Pfeiffer); Victor Malafronte/Celebrity Photo (Donahue). Illustrations by Tom Gammill.
Page 110: John Paschal/Celebrity Photo (Lowe); Patrick McMullan (Wenner); Marina Garnier (Dr. Ruth).
Page 111: Eric Robert/Sygma (Stallone); Victor Malafronte/Celebrity Photo (Kennedy Jr.); Scott Downie/Celebrity Photo (Slater); Marina Garnier (Gere).
Page 112: Smeal/Galella, Ltd. (Schwarzenegger); Patrick McMullan (Hernandez); Marina Garnier (Sawyer, Guest).
Page 113: Aubrey Reuben/London Features Intl. (Rossellini); Patrick McMullan (Kennedy Jr.); AP/Wide World Photos (Dukakis).
Page 114: Smeal/Galella, Ltd. (Kasem); Bauer/Galella, Ltd. (Madonna); Kevin Winter/DMI (Willis); Marina Garnier (O'Rourke).
Page 115: John Paschal/Celebrity Photo (Leach); Aubrey Reuben/London Features Intl. (Stern); Scott Downie/Celebrity Photo (Aykroyd); Ron Galella, Ltd. (Karan).
Page 116: Bauer/Galella, Ltd. (Byrd); Ron Galella, Ltd. (Jones); Marina Garnier (Turner).
Page 117: Marina Garnier (Campbell); Mark Weiss/MWA (Hahn); Ron Galella, Ltd. (Cher).
Page 118: Marina Garnier (Bass, Ono); Ron Galella, Ltd. (top Lebowitz, Letterman, Nicholson); Kevin Winter/DMI (Clay); Patrick McMullan (bottom Lebowitz); John Simone (McInerney).
Page 119: Kevin Winter/DMI (Clay); Aubrey Reuben/London Features Intl. (Turner); Marina Garnier (De Niro); Scott Downie/Celebrity Photo (Williams).
Page 120: Bauer/Galella, Ltd. (Trump, Stewart, Jones); Jordan/Galella, Ltd. (Alexis); Ron Galella, Ltd. (Cavett, Wolfe); Rose Hartman (Rosenthal); Marina Garnier (Gottfried, Buckley).
Page 121: Bob Evans/LGI (Smith); Aubrey Reuben/London Features Intl. (Patinkin); Ron Galella, Ltd. (Koch); Marina Garnier (Reed); AP/Wide World Photos (Dukakis).
Page 122: Marina Garnier (Fox, Richards); Ron Galella, Ltd. (Hannah); AP/Wide World Photos (Dukakis).
Page 123: Aubrey Reuben/London Features Intl. (Ivana Trump); Ron Galella, Ltd. (Douglas); Smeal/Galella, Ltd. (Zadora); Marina Garnier (Steinberg, Blaine Trump, Alt, Norville).
Page 128: Ron Galella, Ltd. (Hawn, Spielberg, Trump); John Paschal/Celebrity Photo (Pop); Janet Gough/Celebrity Photo (Winger).

SPY mascot and school background photos by Sara Barrett.
Spot illustrations by T.P. Moynihan.

Show us your nose hairs! (junior Iggy Pop)

Spy High
Simon Says:

Pretend you're listening to George Will talk! (senior Eddie Murphy)

Cover your ears! (senior Steve Spielberg)

Stick out your tongue! (sophomore Debra Winger)

Make a fish face! (sophomore Martin Short)

Pretend you're Donald Trump! (sophomore Goldie Hawn)

"F.U.—who's Simon? I'm more powerful than him any day." (senior Donald Trump)